AIRBORNE

In this companion volume to *Skyriders*, Alan C. Jenkins has assembled an exciting anthology of true and imaginary adventures in the air. Famous fliers give their first-hand accounts of pioneering solo flights and near-disasters. Bomber pilots carry their cargo of death in a new and terrible kind of warfare. Gaily-painted air balloons drift lazily through the clouds. "Barnstormers" risk their necks in the name of entertainment. Early science fiction writers offer far-fetched and sometimes prophetic visions of how aircraft will change the world. UFOs cross the skies on unfathomable missions.

Francis Chichester, Charles Lindbergh, Sheila Scott, Jules Verne, Liam O'Flaherty, and Rudyard Kipling are some of the celebrated authors and aviators included in this collection of the brave, bizarre, or foolhardy feats of airborne men and women.

AIRBORNE

Compiled by ALAN C. JENKINS

Blackie: Glasgow and London

ISBN 0 216 90047 6
Blackie and Son Limited
Bishopbriggs, Glasgow G64 2NZ
5 Fitzhardinge Street, London W1H 0DL

Printed in Great Britain by
Robert MacLehose and Company Limited, Glasgow

Filmset by Doyle Photosetting Limited, Tullamore, Ireland

To Nan with love

Contents

Acknowledgements

For permission to reprint copyright material I have to thank the following:

The Longman Group Ltd for a passage from *Bird Flight* by Otto Lilienthal, translated by A. W. Isenthal;

The Oxford University Press for a passage from *Other Worlds* by Cyrano de Bergerac, translated by Geoffrey Strachan;

Elleston Trevor for his "Devil Disc";

The Author and Weidenfeld & Nicholson and Arthur Barker for a passage from *Flying Daredevils of the Roaring Twenties* by Don Dwiggins;

John Murray (Publishers) Ltd for a passage from *The Spirit of St Louis* by Charles A. Lindbergh;

Curtis Brown Ltd for a passage from "Bengal Lancer" by F. Yeats-Brown;

Michael Joseph for a passage from *Enemy Coast Ahead* by Guy Gibson;

J. M. Dent & Sons Ltd for a passage from *From the Earth to the Moon* by Jules Verne, translated by Jacqueline Baldick;

Mrs George Bambridge and Macmillan of London and Macmillan of Canada for "With the Night Mail" by Rudyard Kipling;

The Author and Hodder & Stoughton Ltd for a passage from *I Must Fly* by Sheila Scott;

Allen & Unwin Ltd and John Farquharson Ltd for an extract from *Alone Over the Tasman Sea* by Sir Francis Chichester;

Robert de la Croix for a passage from his "Mysteries of the North Pole";

The Author and B.P.C. for a passage from *The Blitz* by Constantine FitzGibbon;

The Macmillan Publishing Co. Inc. for "The Airstrip at Konora" from *Tales of the South Pacific* by James A. Michener;

The Literary Executor and Penguin Books Ltd for a passage from the late Gavin Maxwell's *Ring of Bright Water* (Allen Lane 1974) © 1960, 1974;

The Author and Rupert Hart-Davis (Granada Publishing Ltd) for "Satellite Passage" by Theodore L. Thomas from *S. F. The Best of the Best* (1968) ed. Judith Merrill;

Jonathan Cape Ltd for "His First Flight" from *The Short Stories of Liam O'Flaherty*;

Every effort has been made to trace the ownership of selections included in this anthology in order to secure permission to reprint copyright material and to make full acknowledgement of their use. If any error of omission has occurred, it is purely inadvertent and will be corrected in subsequent editions upon written notification to the publisher, Blackie and Son Ltd, Wester Cleddens Road, Bishopbriggs, Glasgow, G64 2NZ.

Introduction

Airborne is more a companion to *Skyriders* than a continuation of it. For neither of these anthologies sets out to be a chronological history of flying, but each presents a wide and varied cross-section of the enormous thought and effort man put into his attempts to conquer the air: his age-old hankering to fly, expressed in fantasy long before he started practical experiments with flying-machines; his courage in challenging an unfamiliar element; and his dogged refusal to be beaten by it in spite of all the hazards involved.

Although they were generally regarded as madmen by their fellows, these pioneers refused to be put off by the derision and scepticism that surrounded their attempts. "Nothing can compare with the joy that filled me as I flew away from the surface of the earth," Professor Charles wrote in 1783 after his successful balloon flight. "It was not a pleasure, it was blissful delight. After the atrocious sufferings, the persecution and slander I had undergone, I felt that I gave the right answer when I rose above everything. This feeling was quickly replaced by another, still more vivid sensation of admiration for the majestic spectacle that unfolded before our eyes. Wherever we turned our gaze, we saw the heads of people, above us a sky free from cloud, and, in the distance, the most alluring view in the world. I would have liked to shout to my critics, 'Look now, you poor devils, see what risks being destroyed when the progress of science is obstructed!'"

But the progress of science was not obstructed, thanks to the vision of such pioneers, including the professor himself, Otto Lilienthal, the Wright Brothers, and all the many others. Even the dreamers of dreams, such as de Bergerac and Jules Verne, played their part in stimulating man's determination to fly, and their fantasies culminated in the moon-landings that have become so familiar to us. Perhaps "culminated" is not the right word, for brilliant achievements though the moonshots were, they are not the culmination of man's ambitions in the air. His fantasies and his technical feats continue and perhaps in generations to come even such an accomplishment as reaching the moon will be looked back upon as a mere stepping-stone to the far greater limits to which man may be able to reach.

Perhaps there are no limits—and that's the catch!

A. C. J.

Birdman

GUSTAV LILIENTHAL

The idea of flying with artificial wings, as opposed to using a powered machine, has intrigued men ever since the legendary Daedalus. In the nineteenth century, Otto Lilienthal was one of the most persistent enthusiasts and his researches, like those of da Vinci, whose notebooks he must have read, were based on the flight of birds. But like Icarus, he too went to his death in attempting to fly. Nowadays, would-be "birdmen" are devotees of the latest craze of "hang-gliding".

Otto and I were amongst those upon whom enthusiasm for the possibility of flying seized at an early age. A story which was then much-read powerfully stimulated our susceptible minds—"The travels of Count Zambeccay", about an aeronaut, who finally lost his life on the occasion of one of his balloon journeys.

More particularly was our interest awakened by the detailed description and instruction which, in the language of an animal fable, the stork imparts to the willow-wren.

The small willow-wren happens to meet the stork, and complains of fatigue; the latter in his generosity offers him a seat on his back, and during the ensuing conversation the stork explains the method by which he sails without effort or wing-beats, and how he planes down in a straight line from a great altitude to a distant meadow.

13

This clear description of sailing flight impressed us with the possibility of attaining such by simple means. Anklam, our native town, with its surrounding meadows, gave us ample opportunities for observation, since numerous families of storks had taken up their abode on the roofs of the barns, and we often watched the flight of the big, handsome birds. Frequently we would stalk a bird to within a very short distance, and that with the wind, as the stork's sense of smell is small; but on suddenly perceiving us the bird would rise, hopping in our direction until sufficiently lifted by the force of his wings.

Even at that time it became obvious to us that rising *against* the wind must be easier than *with* the wind, because without some compelling cause the shy bird would not advance towards us. In the interests of our aeronautical studies we took a number of young storks from their nests so that we could more easily study them. A young stork from the nest can be readily brought up on meat and fish, and soon gets attached to his keeper.

When the actual flying practice begins, the first attention is devoted to the determination of wind-direction; all the stork's exercises are practised against the wind, but since the latter is not so constant on the lawn as on the roofs, progress is somewhat slower. Frequently, a sudden squall produces eddies in the air, and it is most amusing to watch the birds dancing about with uplifted wings in order to catch the wind which changes from one side to another, all round. Any successful short flight is announced by joyful manifestations. When the wind blows uniformly from an open direction over the clearing, the young stork meets it, hopping and running; then turning round, he gravely walks back to the starting-point and again tries to rise against the wind.

Such exercises are continued daily. At first only one single wing-beat succeeds, and before the wings can be raised for the second beat, the long, cautiously placed legs are again touching ground. But as soon as this stage is passed, i.e. when a second wing-beat is possible without the legs touching the ground, progress becomes very rapid, because the increased forward velocity facilitates flight, and three, four, or more double beats follow each other in one attempt, maybe awkward and unskilled, but never attended by accident, because of the caution exercised by the bird.

While we thus studied the flight of the stork, we continued with our plans to construct a "flying-machine". Our first wings measured two metres by one metre, and consisted of thin beech veneer with straps at the undersides, through which we pushed our arms. It was our intention to run down a hill and to rise against the wind like a stork. In order to escape the jibes of our schoolmates, we experimented at night-time on the drill ground outside the town, but there being no wind on these clear, starlit summer nights, we met with no success.

We were then thirteen and fourteen years of age respectively, and our flying experiments rather interfered with the proper discharge of our school work. However, Otto was sent to the Provincial Technical School at Potsdam and here he was able to satisfy his thirst for technical knowledge, and after a lapse of two years he passed the final examination with the highest honours ever attained.

We had no associate in our aviation experiments; we felt ourselves quite equal to the task. During the vacations we returned to our old hunting-grounds in our desire to study the flight of birds. Buzzards, hawks, rooks and storks interested us most, and great was our delight when we saw a flock of swans outlined against the sky on their migration to their northern breeding-haunts.

My brother left Potsdam for Berlin, and for one year

worked as mechanic at the machine works of Schwarzkopf. He soon proved his great skill in precision work and was later on sent to the Technical Academy. But before the beginning of the first term he paid us a month's visit at Anklam.

He brought with him a bundle of palisander sticks, which were intended for Flying-Machine No. 2. To work the hard palisander wood was no small matter: we pointed and rounded the sticks which served as quills for two wings, each three metres long. The feathers of these quills were represented by a series of large goose feathers which were sewn on tape.

For this purpose we had purchased all the feathers which were obtainable, and this is no mean accomplishment in any Pomeranian town where so many are used commercially.

The sewing on of these quills was very troublesome and tiring for our fingers, and many a drop of blood upon white feathers testified to the damage done to our hands.

The wings were fastened to two hoops, one of which was strapped round the chest, and the other round the hips, and by means of an angle-lever and stirrup arrangement to the ropes we were enabled to beat the wings up and down by pushing out our legs. The single feathers were arranged to open and close on the up- and downstroke, and the arrangement worked perfectly. We felt sure that this time failure was impossible. We believed that the lofty garret of our house in Anklam would be the most suitable experimenting room, a belief which was unfortunate, since we undertook to fly in a perfect calm, a method which presents difficulties even to the bird.

We did not heed the lesson taught by our storks, but suspended our apparatus from the beams of the roof and began to move the wings. The very first movement of our legs caused the suspension rope to jerk, and as our position was nearly horizontal we were most uncomfortable. When drawing up our legs, that is, when the wings moved upwards, the whole contraption dropped down and hung on the taut rope. The lifting effect due to the downward beating of the wings amounted to twenty centimetres. This was at least some success, but if our house had not possessed that high loft, we should have experimented in the open, and with a fresh wind would have recorded better results. But the holidays were at an end, and Flying-Machine No. 2 was relegated to the lumber-room.

In 1868 I joined my brother in Berlin, where we continued our experiments. The first thing we bought was a large bundle of willow canes with which to construct Flying-Machine No. 3. We had abandoned the use of hard palisander wood, because experiments showed us that weight for weight the round willow cane possessed the greatest resistance against breakage, so long as its surface was intact, and that even with the latter defective, it still held together.

We constructed an apparatus consisting of a double system of wings: a pair of wide wings in the centre, and a narrower pair in front and behind, these mounted so as to revolve around a horizontal axis, and so connected that the wings on one side ascended when those on the other side descended, and vice versa. Since the two narrow wings together equalled in area the broader middle wing, we obtained on each side the same lifting area. There was also a "feathering" action, which permitted the air to pass through the wings on their upstroke. Instead of the expensive quills, we employed strips of shirting sewn to the tips of the willow canes.

The whole apparatus had an area of sixteen square metres and weighed only fifteen kilogrammes. By alternately pushing down the feet, one half of the wing area descended and the other ascended against little resistance. The whole machine was suspended by means of a rope and pulleys from a beam, and was counterbalanced by a weight. If the counterweight was heavy enough we could lift ourselves by beating the wings.

This arrangement permitted us to determine the amount of "lift" produced with such an apparatus moved by man-power, and to ascertain the resulting air resistance. After a little practice we were able to lift our weight, so that a forty kilogramme counterweight sufficed to balance the machine and operator, weighing together eighty kilo-grammes. The necessary effort, however, was so great that we could maintain ourselves at a certain level only for a few seconds.

Since we could not very well put up this apparatus in our lodgings, we took it to Demnitz, an estate near Anklam belonging to an uncle of ours—who constantly prophesied disaster.

Our experiments were interrupted by the war of 1870–71 between France and Prussia, in which Otto served. But his enthusiasm was greater than ever when he returned and his first words were, "Now we shall finish it".

We had now come to the conclusion that flight would be impossible without forward motion, and all the experiments which we made on small models were based upon the principle of forward motion. We possessed an apparatus which was fitted with beating wings, moved by spiral springs, and which was launched from an inclined plane out of the window of our lodging on the fourth floor, at four o'clock in the morning, so as to avoid being seen.

The centre of gravity of this apparatus was too low, and the resulting pendulum movements brought the wings al-most into a vertical position and to rest; the apparatus swung back and in consequence of the oblique position of the feather-shaped "valves" it took a second and third start until the spring had run down. This experiment for the first time taught us the importance of the proper position of the centre of gravity.

The best of our various models was fitted with two pigeon's wings; it was able to make twenty wing-beats when the spring was wound up, and when pushed off gently, flew across two rooms.

It was not until 1874 that we resumed our work on flight. In our loft we installed a regular workshop and laid the keel of a wing flyer. The wings were an exact copy of a bird's wings: the pinions consisting of willow canes with narrow front and wide back feathers. The latter we made of corrugated paper steeped in a solution of gum arabic, and after drying, it was covered with collodion. The whole apparatus was the size of a stork, and the propelling force was to be a light motor which, however, had first to be designed. It was on this occasion that Otto, who was experienced in the designing of steam-engines, invented a system of tubular boilers, then quite new. The engine was provided with a high and a low pressure cylinder, the former for the downstroke and the latter for the upstroke of the wings. I believe we should have succeeded in making the model fly, if the motor had not been too powerful, but at the very first trial both wings were broken, not being strong enough to withstand the increased air pressure due to the beating motion.

Still, we were not discouraged by this accident, which we considered as a success for the small motor. The latter with some water and a supply of spirit weighed 0.75 kilogramme and had an output of $\frac{1}{4}$ (one-quarter) hp. We also built kites in the form of birds, in order to study the behaviour of the apparatus in the wind, the surfaces of the wings being curved, in imitation of a bird. Such a kite, which we flew on the high plain between the Spandau road and the railway to Hamburg, showed some peculiar properties. It was held by three persons, one of whom took hold of the two lines which were fastened to the front cane and the tail respectively, while the other two persons each held the line which was fastened to either wing. In this way it was possible to regulate the floating kite, as regards its two axes.

Once, during a very strong wind, we were able so to direct the kite that it moved against the wind. As soon as its long axis was approximately horizontal the kite did not come down but moved forward at the same level. I held the cords controlling the longitudinal axis, and Otto and my sister each one of the cords for the adjustment of the cross-axis. As the kite maintained its lateral equilibrium, they let go the cords; the kite then stood almost vertically above me and I also had to free it.

After I had gone another thirty paces my cords got entangled in some bushes, the kite lost its balance and, in coming down, was destroyed. Yet, having thus gained new experience, we did not feel too badly the loss of model No. 4.

A long absence in Australia now intervened and when we did eventually take up our flying experiments again Otto was particularly keen to compare the actual lifting powers of large curved surfaces with the values which we had determined by measurements. These supporting surfaces are now generally termed "gliders" and we were able to glide slowly downward against the wind from a height. In 1894 we had had constructed, at considerable expense, a special hill, fifteen metres high, at the Heinersdorfer Brickworks near Gross-Lichterfelde. The summit of the hill was formed by a shed in which our "gliders" were stored.

In the meantime we had discovered a very suitable ground near Rinow and Stöllen. On it were a number of bare sandhills rising to a height of fifty metres above the surrounding plain, and from this starting point my brother succeeded in making glides of up to 350 metres. The starting- or take-off-point was at only half the height of the hill, because at the summit the wind was generally too strong. According to my observations the drop of this gliding flight amounted to eighteen metres.

On the occasion of one such flight, one of the supports for the arm broke, so that the apparatus lost its balance and fell from a height of fifteen metres, but the special shock-absorber which was fitted to the apparatus prevented Otto from getting seriously hurt. By 1896 we had three years of such flights behind us and in my opinion we could not expect any better results. We therefore intended to take up experiments with an apparatus fitted with beating wings, the latter being moved by means of a carbonic acid motor.

We had already tested the apparatus as a mere glider without a motor, the latter requiring some improvements. Otto was of the opinion that these gliding flights would develop into a sport. He was indefatigable in this and also in the search for greater security. Moreover, we hoped to derive some pecuniary benefit from these gliding experiments, for they had involved us in great expense, far more than we could afford. So we had agreed that on Sunday 9th August we should travel to Stöllen for the last time in order to bring back the apparatus.

But I was prevented from going on this last trip, and Otto drove out to Stöllen accompanied only by a servant. He decided to have one last flight, as he intended to make some change to the rudder, but at the very first glide, the wind being uncertain, the apparatus lost its balance when at a considerable height.

Unfortunately my brother had not fitted the shock-absorber and the full shock of the fall took effect, so that the apprehensions of our uncle were fulfilled. Otto was killed, a victim of the great idea of flying, which, although at that time so little recognized, is now acknowledged in its full significance by the whole civilized world. Therefore, whenever the laurels of success are attained by an aviator of the present day, let him remember with gratitude the work of Otto Lilienthal!

Recipe for an Air Balloon

ANON

> *But the first practical flying machine was the balloon. The pioneer Montgolfier brothers even tried to sell their invention to the French Army, then at war with Britain — "We possess a superhuman means of introducing soldiers into the impregnable fortress of Gibraltar. By making a large enough bag it will be possible to introduce an entire army, which, borne by the wind, will enter right above the heads of the English." That was in 1782.*

From the nature of air we find that any factitious air which is lighter than the atmosphere ascends. We see this by that air which is produced by a fire, called smoke, which being specifically lighter than the atmospheric air, is carried up the chimney, and only settles when it gets to that height which is equal to its own levity. This quality of air has been long understood, and various theories have been suggested to what purpose it may be applied; though Monsieur Montgolfier, we believe, was the first European philosopher who made it a "travelling convenience" for man, and gave to the world an experiment which is likely to become as useful as it is at present curious.

The method of making the air which fills this *Aerostatic Globe* is as follows:

Take a certain quantity of oil of vitriol, in the proportion of an ounce to a quart of water, and mix both with filings of iron: these produce a factitious air, supposed to be about ten times lighter than the atmosphere. This air so made is by a tube conducted into the *Air Balloon* so as not to give it all the fullness of a common bladder, but rather loose in some parts, and this keeps it the longer from bursting in its progress through the air. The form of the *Air Balloon* is orbicular, or round—it is generally made of taffeta, or thin silk, on account of its lightness, and gummed on the seams, the better to prevent the air from transpiring.

When it is properly filled, it is closely tied at the end, and from this moment it becomes so much a lighter body than the circumambient air, that it would immediately ascend, if not restrained by a proportionate balance. When it is let off (which is done by cutting the strings which restrain it) it rises for some time perpendicular, and rather slowly; it then follows the direction of the wind in a progressive ascent, till it reaches that region of the air which is lighter than itself. This air repels it with that force, so as either to burst it, or to force out by degrees the factitious air; in either case, it descends with rapidity to the earth.

From this method of using an *Air Balloon*, the Public will readily see that the experiment can only gratify curiosity—as very little or no use can be made of it, there being no possibility of restraining its height, or preventing its rapid declension—in either case it must be fatal to any person to ascend with it, as it may travel through regions of air too rarefied for human respiration, and fall with such rapidity as to crush him to pieces.

To remedy this, the same ingenious inventor has adopted another method of filling his *Balloon* by which he has secured its ascent and descent with more certainty and safety; which is, instead of oil of vitriol, water, and filings of iron, to make his air of that smoke which is produced by the burning of wet straw, and by carrying a quantity of this fuel with him (in a little gallery constructed round the *Balloon*, for the purpose of feeding it) he can ascend or descend at pleasure.

The method of supplying this last *Balloon* with air is, by burning the straw on a grate affixed to the bottom of it—the smoke of which is infused into the *Balloon* by a tube, to which there is a cock to let it out as occasions may require.

On this he has made several experiments in the presence of many thousands of spectators in Paris; amongst whom were some of the first rank in life and letters. But the greatest experiment which has as yet been made was that on the 19th of October last by the Sieur Giroud de Villette and Monsieur Rozier. The *Balloon* constructed for this purpose was sixty feet long and forty broad, which being filled with air made by the smoke of wet straw was capable of taking up these two enterprising Philosophers, together with the weight of the gallery attached to it, and several pounds weight of fuel.

They took the opportunity of a day when the wind blew across the city of Paris, and ascending at one side Port St. Jacques, crossed over to the Faubourg St. Martin, that is, by way of making it more familiar to an English ear (supposing the experiment was made in London), as if they ascended at St. George's Fields, and traversing across the city, came down in one of the fields near Islington.

The height they ascended was made by a computation, which was taken as they passed over the church of St. Sulpice, and is said to be 1650 feet, which is more than four times higher than St. Paul's. In this region (contrary to the received opinion of most philosophers, that man could not live in such rarefied air) they could breathe freely; and so supported were they by the enthusiasm of their enterprise, that they had resolution enough to enjoy the bird's-eye prospect of so stupendous a height and clearly see Neuilly, St. Cloud, Sèvrs, Iffy, Ivry, Charenton, and Choisy—some of those places forty-eight miles from the capital. The gardens about Paris appeared to them like bouquets, and the people passing and re-passing (according to the strong expression of Monsieur Rozier) "like so many mites in a cheese"—no bad situation to humble the pride of man and make him feel his individual littleness and insignificancy in the great scale of Creation.

In respect to the weight an *Air Balloon* can carry, it must depend on the size. That constructed by Mr Biaggini, and lately let off in the Artillery Ground, Moorfields, was ten feet in diameter, and could have carried about sixteen pounds* — so that by a computation of this kind, on a more enlarged scale, the exact weight can be readily ascertained. That lately sent up in Paris, which we have been just describing, was sixty feet long, and forty broad—and must have carried up (computing the weight of the two men, the gallery, and straw) not less than between three and four hundredweights.

In respect to its rate of travelling in the air, we may very well suppose it at least fifteen miles an hour from the average calculation of experiments which have been made, without allowing for the loss of time in the perpendicular ascent, and the obstructions it is subject to meet with from the shiftings of the wind; and if in any future discovery we should be able to direct its course, there is no doubt it will travel with still more velocity.

Such is a brief and plain description of an *Air Balloon*, which has with so much justice roused the curiosity and attention of all Europe—a discovery, we must confess, hitherto merely curious, but which bids fair, from the probable improvements which may be made in it, to be highly serviceable to society.

*Mr Biaggini has just now prepared another *Air Balloon*, which he is exhibiting at the Pantheon, and which he shortly intends to let off in the Artillery Ground, 16-feet diameter, and of force sufficient to carry up a child of eight years old.

Recipe for an Air Balloon

At present, however, by this invention we can only ascend and descend, and the latter, perhaps, not always with the most perfect security; it is, besides, at the mercy of the wind, "to be blown with restless violence round about this pendent world", as Shakespeare has it. The first object of improvement, therefore, will be to direct its motion in the air by the means of wings, or feathered oars. This may appear visionary to some; but we have authority to assure the Public, that not only the original inventor of the *Air Balloon* is busied in this project, but something of a similar nature is now in great forwardness amongst ourselves, under the direction of a Scotch artist, who is already supported by a subscription of seven hundred guineas to complete it.

The machine is to be in the form of a bird; the body is to contain the inflammable air; the shaft of the wings to be nine feet long, and nine inches wide; both to be made of the purest elastic steel ever wrought in this country, and the whole is to be worked and directed by a person who is to go up in a basket attached to the machine.

This once obtained, the uses which might arise from it are many and various.

On the first report of a country being invaded, an *Air Balloon* would save the expenses of messengers, posts, etc. from the coasts to the main army, as at the height it ascends, with the assistance of glasses, the number of the enemy, together with their place of landing, might be communicated with great dispatch.

A general, likewise, in the day of battle would derive singular advantage by going up in one of these machines; he would have a bird's-eye view not only of everything that was doing in his own, but also the enemy's army, and by sending down his orders occasionally (which may be done by the means of a plummet) he may literally be said "To ride in the whirlwind, and direct the storm."

Observations at sea may likewise be made at a greater distance, and with a greater certainty than at present, which would not only be useful in time of war, and preventive of accidents at all times, but add perhaps extensive discoveries to our terrestrial globe.

During sieges they may be rendered particularly useful, by observing the works of the enemy and, of course, rendering them ineffectual. Had this discovery been known even so late as the siege of Gibraltar, it would have saved that brave garrison some lives, and great labour, as occasional turrets were obliged to be built the better to observe the operations of the enemy—all which an *Air Balloon* would have saved. In cases of fires in capitals or large towns, an *Air Balloon* let off would instantly ascertain where the fire was, and of course occasion a more direct and speedy assistance.

To maintain a war of posts, as was pretty much the case in the late war in America, an *Air Balloon* would be of the most singular advantage. For instance, had the troops in that unfortunate expedition to Albany been provided with this celebrated discovery, to give necessary signals and intelligence to the detachment who were to support them, the effects of that unfortunate day would not be recorded, as they now are, in the debilitated and humiliating state of Great Britain.

In Natural Philosophy it bids fair to make many great and considerable improvements. It is well known that our great philosopher Dr Franklyn, by means of an artificial *Kite*, has already drawn down lightning from the clouds. Why may not this experiment be improved by means of an *Air Balloon*? When the appearance and approach of clouds prognosticate immediate thunder, an *Air Balloon* carrying up conductors might draw it down, and separate that force, which oft has proved fatal to the lives of many. In the West and East Indies, where thunderstorms are infinitely more frequent and mischievous than in these countries, it would be a discovery of the most salutary kind, and as its objects would be of such material advantage to the natives, there is little doubt but such further improvements may be made, as the very bad effects of thunder may in a great measure be prevented.

Physics may keep equal pace with the other improvements in Natural Philosophy: for as the great organs of our senses, tasting, feeling, hearing, and smelling, are communicated to us through the medium of the air, who can say what improvements the constitution might receive from such quick and elevated changes? We all know that some invalids are only kept alive by what physicians call the "change of air", that is, by travelling from one country or town to another—but as the air is always allowed to be purer in its ascent, and as an *Air Balloon* can regulate that ascent to precision, the benefits may be of the most valuable kind. In asthmas and decays, it may turn out a specific, and in other diseases, though not so powerful, yet highly serviceable.

In short, as the various properties of air are at present so well known to contribute to the preservation of our existence, what are we not led to hope from a knowledge of using it, and living in it in a purer and more extensive degree than ever? The present period seems to be a favourable omen for the extension and encouragement of this discovery—as Peace, the parent and patron of all knowledge, has happily once more revisited Europe, and calls upon its philosophers and artists to erase the ravages of war, by the cultivation of useful and ornamental science, as exampled in the *Air Balloon*.

Since writing the above, the Editor is favoured with a letter from a respectable correspondent in Paris, dated 3rd December, acquainting him of a late experiment made of the *Air Balloon*, which he is happy in laying before the public, as it in a great measure justifies the sanguine hopes he entertains of its further improvement.

Thus: On Monday 1st December an *Air Balloon*, under the direction of Messrs Charles and Roberts, was let off from the Tuileries. It had suspended to it a basket, covered with blue silk and paper finely gilt, in the shape of a triumphal car, in which Mr Charles and Mr Roberts embarked, and mounted up into the air, amidst many thousands of people of all ranks and conditions, perhaps three or four hundred thousand all. Beside the Duke of Chartres and a great part of the French nobility there were the Duke and Duchess of Cumberland, the Duke and Duchess of Manchester, and many other foreign princes and nobility. The philosophers had flags with them of different colours, with which, as they mounted aloft, they saluted the admiring world below. When they came to the height at which they meant to sail (which was computed to be about twice the height of St. Paul's) they threw down a flag as agreed. They then glided along a steady horizontal track over the Faubourg St. Honoré, saluting the people as they went along, with their flags; and landed at about twenty miles' distance from the place they set out from, being accompanied (*sur la terre*) by the Duke of Chartres, and several of the French and English nobility and gentry, who came in almost at their landing. Mr Roberts then got out, when Mr Charles, after throwing out some ballast to lighten the machine, ascended alone in the *Balloon* to the almost incredible height of 15,026 *toises*, or 3,052 yards perpendicular, in about ten minutes.

The account Mr Charles gives of his observations during this time is, that he lost sight of everything below upon earth, and saw nothing but a wide expanse of fine ether—that the Barometer fell from 28 to 18, and the Thermometer from 7 above freezing to 5 below it. He descended about four or five miles from the spot he got up, near the house of a Mr Farrar, an English gentleman, where he slept that night, and was brought to town by a nobleman in his own carriage the next day, amidst the general acclamations of the Public.

The *Balloon* was composed of red and straw-coloured taffeta, which were pieced alternately, so as to appear like meridional lines upon a terrestrial globe. The upper hemisphere was covered with a netting, surrounded at the bottom by a hoop, to which the car was suspended; so that the elastic pressure of the inflammable air was equally repressed by all the meshes of the net above. Monsieur Montgolfier attended during the experiment.

We are sorry to add to this account, that on the arrival of Messrs Charles and Roberts in Paris, they were arrested by order of the King, who, as "father of his people", was advised by some bigoted Ecclesiastics to prevent the farther endangering the lives of his subjects. But as great interest is making for them by the princes of the blood, together with all the philosophers in Paris, it is thought they will speedily be discharged. Public curiosity is much damped by this circumstance, as the next experiment Mr Charles meant to make of the *Air Balloon* was to take a trip in it from Calais to Dover, in which he was to be accompanied by the celebrated Monsieur Bougainville, the first French circumnavigator of the world.

Journey to the Moon

CYRANO DE BERGERAC

Soldier, wit, student of philosophy, poet and rake, there were many facets to the character of de Bergerac, who lived in France from 1619–55. He was a brilliant, if erratic person, and had ideas on paper for a balloon, a parachute, a rocket-ship, and even a gramophone. Although he sub- titled the book from which this passage comes, The Comical History of the States and Empires of the Moon and Sun, *his idea of lunar travel has materialized, as we know, though by slightly different methods than his!*

The moon was full, the sky was cloudless, and it had already struck nine. We were returning from Clamard, near Paris, where the younger Monsieur de Cuigy, who is the squire there, had been entertaining myself and several of my friends. Along the road we amused ourselves with the various speculations inspired by this ball of saffron. All our eyes were fixed on the great star. One of our number took it for a garret window in heaven, through which the glory of the blessed could be glimpsed. Another, convinced by the fables of the ancients, thought it possible that Bacchus kept a tavern up there in the heavens and that he had hung up the full moon as a sign. Another assured us that it was the round, copper ironing-board on which Diana presses Apollo's collars. Another that it might be the Sun itself, having cast off its rays in the evening, watching through a peep-hole to see what happened on Earth in its absence.

"And as for me," I told them, "I will gladly add my own contribution to your transports. I am in no way diverted by the ingenious fancies with which you flatter time, to make it pass more quickly, and I believe that the Moon is a world like ours, which our world serves as a moon."

Some of the company treated me to a great outburst of laughter. "And that, perhaps," I said to them, "is just how someone else is being ridiculed at this very moment in the Moon for maintaining that this globe here is a world."

But although I informed them that Pythagoras, Epicurus, Democritus, and, in our own age, Copernicus and Kepler had been of the same opinion, I merely made them laugh more heartily.

Nevertheless this notion, the boldness of which matched the humour I was in, was only fortified by contradiction and lodged so deeply in my mind that for all the rest of the day I remained pregnant with a thousand definitions of the moon, of which I could not be delivered. As a result of upholding this fanciful belief with half-serious arguments, I had almost reached the stage of yielding to it, when there came the miracle—the accident, stroke of fortune, chance (you may well name it vision, fiction, chimera or, if you will, madness) —which afforded me the opportunity that has engaged me upon this account.

Upon my arrival home I went up to my study, where I found a book open on the table, which I had certainly not put there myself. It was that of Girolamo Cardano* and, although I had had no intention of reading from it, my eyes seemed to be drawn to the particular story which this philosopher tells of how, when studying one evening by candlelight, he observed the entry, through closed doors, of two tall, old men. After he had put many questions to them,

---

De subtilate rerum by Girolamo Cardano (1501–76), doctor, mathematician, philosopher, and alchemist.

they replied that they were inhabitants of the Moon and at the same moment disappeared. This left me in such amazement—as much at seeing a book which had transported itself there all by itself, as at the occasion when it had happened and the page at which it had been opened—that I took the whole chain of incidents to be a revelation, sent in order that men should know that the Moon is a world.

"How now," I said to myself, "here have I been talking about one thing all day, and now does a book, which is perhaps the only one in the world where this matter is so particularly dealt with, fly from my library to my table, become capable of reason to the extent of opening itself at the very place where just such a marvellous adventure is described, pull my eyes towards it as if by force, and then furnish my imagination with the reflections and my will with the intentions which now occur to me?

"Doubtless," I continued, "the two ancients who appeared to that great man are the very same who have moved my book and opened it at this page, in order to spare themselves the trouble of making me the speech they had already made to Cardano.

"But", I added, "how can I resolve this doubt without going the whole way up there?"

"And why not?" I answered myself at once. "Prometheus went to heaven long ago to steal fire there. Am I less bold than he? And have I any reason not to hope for an equal success?"

After these outbursts, which may perhaps be called attacks of delirium, came the hope that I might successfully accomplish so fine a voyage. In order to make an end of it, I shut myself away in a comparatively isolated country house where, having gratified my daydreams with some practical measures appropriate to my design, this is how I offered myself up to heaven.

I had fastened all about me a quantity of small bottles

filled with dew. The sun beat so violently upon them with its rays that the heat which attracted them, just as it does the thickest mists, raised me aloft until at length I found myself above the middle region of the air. But the attraction made me rise too rapidly and, instead of it bringing me nearer to the moon, as I had supposed it would, this now seemed to me more distant than at my departure. I therefore broke several of my phials, until I felt that my weight was overcoming the attraction and that I was descending towards the Earth again.

My supposition was correct, for I fell to Earth some little time afterwards and, reckoning from the hour at which I had left, it should have been midnight. However, I perceived that the sun was now at its zenith and that it was midday.

I leave you to picture my astonishment. It was very great indeed, and not knowing how to explain this miracle, I was insolent enough to imagine God had favoured my daring by once more nailing the sun to the heavens in order to illuminate an enterprise of such grandeur. I was further astonished by the fact that I completely failed to recognize the country where I found myself. For it seemed to me that, having gone straight up into the air, I should have come down in the place I had left from. However, accoutred as I was, I made my way towards a kind of cottage where I could see some smoke, and I was barely a pistol-shot away from it when I found myself surrounded by a large number of stark-naked men. They seemed greatly surprised to have encountered me, for I was, I believe, the first person dressed in bottles they had ever seen. What still further confounded all the interpretations they might have put upon my harness was to see that I hardly touched the earth as I walked. What they did not know was that at the least impulse I gave to my body, the heat of the noonday rays lifted me up with my dew and if my phials had not been too few in number I could quite

35

easily have been carried away on the winds before their eyes.

I was going to address them but they disappeared in an instant into the near-by forest, just as if fright had turned them all into birds. However, I managed to catch one of them, whose legs had doubtless betrayed his feelings. I asked him with some difficulty (for I was quite out of breath) what the distance was reckoned to be from there to Paris; since when, in France, people went about stark-naked; and why they ran away from me in such alarm. The man to whom I was speaking was an olive-skinned ancient who first of all threw himself at my knees and then clasped his hands in the air behind his head, opened his mouth and closed his eyes. He mumbled between his teeth for a long time but I did not notice that he was articulating anything and took his talk for the husky babblings of a mute.

Some time later I saw a company of soldiery arriving with beating drums and observed two of them emerging from the ranks to investigate me. When they were near enough to be heard, I asked them where I was.

"You are in France, you might say," they answered me. "But what devil has put you in that state and how comes it that we do not know you? Have the ships arrived? Are you going to inform my Lord the Governor? And why have you divided up your brandy into so many bottles?"

To all this I retorted that the devil had certainly not put me in that state I was in; that they did not know me for the reason that they could not know all men; that I knew nothing of the Seine carrying ships to Paris; that I had no message for my Lord the Marshal of the Hospital; and that I carried no brandy at all.

"Oho," they said, taking me by the arm, "so you want to play the clown. My Lord the Governor will know you, all right!"

They led me towards their troop, where I learned that I

was indeed in France—in New France. Some little time later I was presented to the Viceroy, who asked me my country, my name, and my quality. I satisfied him by relating the happy outcome of my voyage and, whether he believed it or only pretended to do so, he had the goodness to arrange for me to be given a room in his house. My joy was great at meeting a man capable of lofty reasoning, who was not at all surprised when I told him that the Earth must have revolved during the course of my levitation, since I had begun my ascent two leagues away from Paris and had come down almost perpendicularly in *Canada*.

During my sojourn in the province I had many highly interesting and philosophical conversations with the Governor, which I have detailed elsewhere. But my intention of ascending to the Moon was more eager than ever and I returned to the project as speedily as possible.

As soon as the moon rose I would go off through the woods, dreaming of the conduct and success of my enterprise; and finally, one Eve of St. John, when a council was being held at the Fort to determine whether help should be given to the local savages against the Iroquois, I went off all alone behind our house to the top of a small hill and here is what I carried out:

I had built a machine which I imagined capable of lifting me as high as I desired and in my opinion it lacked nothing essential. I seated myself inside it and launched myself into the air from the top of a rock. But because my preparations had been inadequate I tumbled roughly into the valley. Covered with bruises as I was, I nevertheless returned from there to my room without losing heart, took some marrow of beef and anointed my whole body with it, for I was battered all over from head to foot. After fortifying my courage with a bottle of a cordial essence, I returned to look for my machine.

I did not find it, however, for some soldiers, who had been sent into the forest to cut wood to build a fire for the feast of St. John, had chanced upon it and brought it to the Fort, where several explanations of what it could be were advanced. When the device of the spring, with which the machine was equipped, was discovered, some said a quantity of rockets should be attached to it, so that when their speed had lifted them high enough and the motor was agitating its great wings, no one could fail to take the machine for a fire dragon.

Meanwhile I spent a long time searching for it, but at last I found it in the middle of the square in Quebec, just as they were setting fire to it. My dismay at discovering my handiwork in such danger so excited me that I ran to seize the arm of the soldier who was setting light to it. I snatched the fuse from him and threw myself furiously into my machine to destroy the contrivance with which it had been surrounded, but I arrived too late, for I had hardly set my two feet inside it when I was borne up into the blue.

The horror which overcame me did not destroy my presence of mind so completely as to make me incapable of recalling later what happened to me at that moment. When the fire had consumed one row of the rockets, which had been arranged six by six, the device of a fuse, fixed at the end of each half-dozen, set off another layer and then another, so that the saltpetre caught fire and gave me a fresh lease of life, at the same time as it carried me further into danger.

However, when the supply was all used up, the contrivance failed and I was resigning myself to leaving my crown upon that of some mountain when (without my making any movement at all) I felt my levitation continuing. My machine took leave of me and I saw it falling back towards the Earth. This extraordinary occurrence filled my heart with a joy so uncommon that in my delight at seeing myself delivered from certain disaster, I had the impudence to philosophize upon it. As I was thus exercising my eyes and my brain to seek out the cause, I noticed my swollen flesh, still greasy with the marrow I had smeared upon myself for the bruises from my tumble. I realized that the moon was on the wane and, just as it is accustomed in that quarter to suck the marrow out of animals,* so it was drinking up what I had smeared upon myself, and with all the more strength because its globe was nearer to me, so that its vigour was in no way impaired by the intervention of clouds.

When, according to the calculations I have since made, I had travelled much more than three-quarters of the way from the Earth to the Moon, I suddenly found myself falling head first, although I had not somersaulted in any fashion. I would not, indeed, have noticed this, if I had not felt my head taking the weight of my body. I was, in fact, quite certain that I was not falling back towards our world, for although I found myself between two moons, I could clearly observe that the farther I went from one, the nearer I came to the other, and I was convinced that the larger one was our globe, since, after I had been travelling for a day or two, the reflected light of the sun grew more distant and gradually the distinctions between different land masses and climates became blurred and it no longer seemed to me like anything other than a great disc of gold. This made me think I was coming down towards the Moon and this supposition was confirmed when I came to remember that I had only begun to fall after three-quarters of the way

"For", I said to myself, "this body, being smaller than our Earth, must have a less extensive sphere of influence and in consequence I have felt the pull of its centre later."

At last, after I had been falling for a very long time—or so

*It was popularly believed that, when the moon was on the wane, the bones of animals contained little or no marrow, since it was sucked out of them by the moon.

I presumed, for the violence of my precipitation made observation difficult—the next thing I can remember is finding myself under a tree, entangled with two or three large branches which I had shattered in my fall, and with my face moist from an apple which had been crushed against it.

The Devil Disc

ELLESTON TREVOR

*A quarter of a century ago, when this story was written, there was a
spate of alleged sightings of "Unidentified Flying Objects", and indeed
claims about U.F.O.'s or Flying Saucers still crop up, while, as we
saw in the* Skyriders *anthology, there have even been picturesque claims
to have met space-folk from other planets who have landed on the Earth.
But ever since stories such as "The Magic Carpet" or "The Enchanted
Horse," men have been indulging in fantasies about the air.*

"Coming in to land . . . Over . . ."

Against the great crimson flush of the sunset, the angular
silhouette of the airport tower. Lowering from the thin racks
of cloud, the shape of the lone *Spitfire*. And the signal,

"Clear to land. You may come in now . . ."

From the watch-tower they heard the lessening note of the
Rolls-Royce engine. From the cockpit of the machine the
pilot looked down to the long runway. His hand moved.
Below the mainplanes the undercarriage swung into position. Then the signal reached the tower,

*"Another machine in circuit. Confirm your all-clear, please . . .
Over!"*

In the tower, Max Browning cocked a look at the signals
man. Clifton shook his head, taking up his binoculars. He
said,

41

"He must be seeing things. Clear him again."

The earphones spoke again into the pilot's ears—

"*No other machine in circuit. All clear to land. All clear to land . . . Over.*"

In the circling *Spitfire*, Vic Spiers narrowed his eyes through the windshield. Dead ahead of him now, the other machine appeared to hover, with the reflection of the sunset streaking the metal fuselage. Vic spoke tersely,

"*You must be blind. Machine ahead of me . . . Over.*"

His hand moved again, twice. The undercarriage swung up slowly; the throttle-lever went forward in its gate. The engine sent out a sudden angry surge that echoed against the watch-tower. Spiers moved up on the other machine, got within 500 yards of it—and then his breath blocked in his throat. The strange machine turned, with a suddenness that made Spiers blink . . . and lifted, with a burst of speed that was uncanny and took it 1000 feet . . . 2000 . . . 3000 feet into the thin cloud-reefs and out of sight.

The signal reached the tower, and the two men there were startled as they heard,

"*Ye gods—it's a disc! It's a flying disc! Stand by—am giving chase! Stand by!*"

Even as the strange call came through to the tower, the men heard the second surge of exhaust-slam from the evening sky, and saw the *Spitfire* go straight into a slight dive and then lift suddenly, rising . . . rising into the frail shelves of cloud until it was lost, and the echoes died. Max Browning jerked out,

"Keep the ass in sight if you can! He's off chasing butterflies . . ."

Clifton was at the windows, binoculars raised.

"I've lost him already—too much cloud. What d'you think he's spotted, a Flying Saucer?"

"Either that—or a machine we couldn't see from down

here. I don't believe in fairies, Father Christmas, or Flying Saucers—"

He was interrupted by the radio—

"*Stand by, Max, and record this: Am climbing at 15,000. Flying disc still ahead of me. Enormous size—looks like polished metal— brilliant blue light now streaming from rim.*"

Browning's pencil was jerking. Clifton stayed by the windows and said nothing. Ten seconds passed, then,

"*18,000 feet. Disc blindingly bright now—seems to be leading me on. Must be enormous size. A giant disc. Am climbing to 20,000 before I—*"

In the tower, silence came. Browning's pencil stopped. Clifton stared at him. Beyond the windows lay the dulling glow of the sunset, a few streamers of cloud, nothing more. Then Browning's hand jerked again, recording,

"*Disc evading me! Sudden swerve to port—blinding streaks of exhaust light—it's climbing rapidly! I haven't a chance to—*" then silence, for five seconds, until—"*Have lost it! Vanished like a lamp going out! Acceleration simply fantastic! Am carrying no oxygen, so will give up . . .*"

For minutes neither Browning nor Clifton spoke, but now their ears caught the loudening hum of the *Spitfire*, and the call came through,

"*Coming in to land. Permission to land, please . . . Over.*"

Max cleared him on the radio. Within five minutes Vic Spiers was home from the twilit sky and striding into the watch-tower. He slung his soft helmet on to a chair-back and grabbed the public telephone. His face was white. His hands shook with excitement. Max said,

"What, no goblins with you, Vic?"

Spiers shot him a quick, impatient glance.

"I was *not* joking," he said grimly.

Clifton watched the owner of the private *Spitfire*, and despite his own scepticism of so-called Flying Saucers he thought, "whatever Spiers saw up there, it's rattled him badly . . ."

Vic was talking, and talking fast, into the phone, "Brainstorm? Vic here. Listen. I'm driving down to see you right away, from Brinton Airfield. I've just had a race with a flying disc—and lost! What? Yes, I can sketch it for you! No, this is no rag, little brother—I've never been more serious in my life! Yes—right away. Expect me within the hour. 'Bye . . ."

He hung up, wheeling to face the two watch-tower men. "What d'you think of that thing, Maxie?"

Max said with a wooden stare, "I didn't see a thing, either that thing or any other. Better sleep it off, Vic."

Spiers stared back, then flashed a glance to Clifton. "You see it, Cliff?"

"Only the sunset, Vic. Nothing else."

The private flyer began unzipping his leather suit, then stopped, picking up his gloves and jerking to the door.

"All right, I'm seeing things . . . If you want me, I'm at my brother's place. So long!"

The slim white Allard slid to a halt, and from a dark saloon two men came over.

"Sorry to hold you up, sir, but are you the pilot of the private *Spitfire* that just landed?"

Vic quizzed them, puzzled. They were in plain clothes, but their manner suggested they were police.

"I am," he said, briefly.

The spokesman nodded. "I've instructions to make a request—that you come with us immediately to Air Security H.Q., Farnborough."

Vic eyed him. "Credentials, gentlemen?"

The taller man produced a wallet, exposing a talc-protected panel. *Flt.Lt. J. F. Walker, Air Security.*

44

"All right, sir?"

Spiers nodded. "All right. You lead the way, I'll tuck in behind." As he slipped into gear he tilted a look at the men. "Did you say 'request'—or 'order'?"

The tall one smiled briefly. "We can only request civilians, sir—and rely on their co-operation . . ."

Vic Spiers, an ex-R.A.F. flyer himself, gave a grin.

"Fair enough," he said.

The white Allard slipped along the winding lane, in the wake of the dark saloon. Turning into the main road, they speeded up, and moved into the sixties behind full headlights. In half an hour Spiers was escorted into a brightly lit office on the ground floor of Air Security H.Q. From behind a crowded desk a stocky man in his forties rose to his feet and covered the visitor with one keen glance.

"All right," he said to the escort. They turned and left, closing the door. The R.A.F. officer held out his hand. "Group-Captain Barnes. And you're Mr V. G. Spiers, I believe."

Vic's fist was gripped by velvet-skinned steel, and he took the chair offered. The Group-Captain resumed his seat.

"Mr Spiers, you own a private *Supermarine Spitfire*, JXM-354, based at Brinton?"

"Correct."

"And this evening you flew in pursuit of an aircraft in the vicinity of the airport?"

"I did. An aircraft I've never dreamed up even in a New Year's Eve nightmare . . . But how did you know?"

"It's a matter of routine. Our job is to know everything that goes on in the sky."

"Then someone else saw that devil disc! One of your boys?"

The Group-Captain gave him a level look.

"No, Mr Spiers. No one else saw it—and neither did you."

Vic's eyes narrowed. When he had been hijacked by the two R.A.F. investigators he had been puzzled. Now he thought he saw daylight.

"I understand, sir. The disc is a secret machine of yours—experimental." But the officer shook his head, his hard blue eyes never leaving Spiers's face.

"No, we had no secret experiment going on anywhere near Brinton this evening. You saw an optical illusion. Either a weird effect of the sunset, reflected glare on a flock of birds, or—"

Vic was on his feet. "Sunset—a flock of birds?" He controlled the excitement in his voice. "Group-Captain Barnes, what I saw was a giant machine with disc-shaped wings that sent out a stream of brilliant blue light—and it manoeuvred ahead of my Spit as if I were flying a leaking bathtub! That was before it vanished like a bat out of blazes and left me squinting at stars!"

The officer's tone was perfectly level.

"An illusion, Mr Spiers."

"An illusion? Which your men saw, too? Otherwise why did they grab me as soon as I left the field? Why did you have me brought here? How d'you know my name, my initials, the number of my kite? Why bother with a crazy flyer who sees gremlins in the sky?"

The Group-Captain did not move. He said,

"For a very good reason. We get many reports of queer phenomena, airborne freaks, unorthodox aircraft. As you know, for the last two years there has been a Flying Saucer scare, and it's been worldwide. Russia says these things are American and British secret weapons. America and Britain say they're Russian secret weapons. Some people say they are spaceships from another planet . . ." He shrugged. "These reports could be dangerous, Spiers. If they got out of hand, they'd cause global panic. Part of our job is to stop them—nip them in the bud where it's possible. That is why I asked you to see me; and that's why I'm asking you this: go away and just forget it. Don't talk about it. You just didn't see anything in the sky tonight ... except a trick of the light."

Vic stood motionless, his brain racing round the puzzle of the flying disc—and the puzzle of this man's attitude. Something was going on, something big. He'd caught a glimpse of it—and he'd been grabbed on the spot.

"You say the thing I saw was no secret experimental aircraft that the R.A.F. knows about?"

"It was not."

"I'd like your personal word for that."

"You have it."

The two men faced each other, the one standing, bewildered, suspicious; the other seated, calm, expressionless. It was deadlock, until the Group-Captain said,

"I'd like your personal word, too, Mr Spiers, that you'll do as I ask. That you'll forget this illusion you saw above Brinton Field. Further, that if you've already told anyone about it, you'll admit to them that you made a mistake."

Vic met the hard blue gaze for a moment, and then shrugged. "In that case, I've no choice. Have I?"

In his stuttering, staccato speech, Vic's younger brother—"Brainstorm" Spiers, assistant astro-physicist at the Southern Cosmic Research Centre—told him what was already known of the so-called Flying Saucers.

"We believe the Earth has been under observation from another planet for the past two centuries ... There are eight hundred reports on record between 1870 and today. They've been carefully checked, and all doubtful and fanciful reports weeded out. The strongest theory's this: another world is watching us. Until World War II, it wasn't interested. Then the Earth started slinging V2's and other rockets about in the sky. The Earth's surface sprouted huge mushrooms at Hiroshima—Nagasaki—the Bikini atoll—and this unknown planet got more interested. That's why the last six years have shown intensified activity of these Flying Saucers—"

"Hold on, Brainstorm!"

The light flashed across the young scientist's spectacles as he turned his copper-haired head. His thin, freckled hands stopped fretting with the papers on his littered desk. Vic said,

"It's a neat theory—but not the only one, surely?"

"The others don't hold water. One: the discs are secret experimental weapons of a Great Power. Answer: no Great Power would chuck its secrets about wholesale; it would keep to its own territory; and these discs have been sighted over almost every country in the world—besides which, flyers who've tried to catch them, as you tried, have said the discs are so huge and so fast that no engine built on Earth could possibly power them. Two: the discs are all illusions—flights of fancy, flights of birds, a trick of light on Met. balloons. Answer: reports have come in from people whose judgement is beyond question—famous names, experienced pilots, professional astronomers. Three: the discs are heavy ice-formations, meteorites, or clouds. Answer: the 'ice' would have to weigh hundreds of tons to be the size observers report the discs to be; meteorites can never fly *upwards*, as the discs do on many occasions; and as for clouds . . . well, was that a cloud you saw this evening?"

Vic said nothing for a while, but his brain rioted. Then he said, quietly, "I told you about Barnes. What d'you make of him?"

Brainstorm leaned back. "I believe part of what he said. The public might panic if the truth came out too suddenly. So it's being allowed to leak out, slowly, so we can get used to the idea of Flying Saucers before we see the headlines right before our eyes . . . You've promised to say nothing about what you saw. But there's nothing to stop you playing a lone game. Go out and hunt that devil disc again if you have the chance. And fit a camera-gun to your *Spit*!"

Vic looked up, and his eyes shone.

"Hunt it again . . . alone!"

His brother nodded. "And bring me the evidence. Between us, we could really find out something . . ."

For three weeks, Vic Spiers hung about Brinton Field, lounging in his machine with the engine warmed, drinking tea with the crew in the watchtower, his eyes on the sky. And nothing happened. He had admitted to Clifton and Browning that he'd been mistaken that night and he took their chaff without a murmur, keeping faith with Group-Captain Barnes.

And then, towards sundown on a clear evening, Max Browning saw something to the west—a line of light. It moved, at a fantastic speed, across the heavens, and then hovered for seconds. Within those few seconds, Vic was sprinting down to his machine, gunning it up, waving the chocks away as his mechanics stared skywards.

At 18.12 hours, 29 March, Vic Spiers's *Supermarine Spitfire* JXM–354 lifted from Brinton Field with full tanks and a primed camera-gun, climbing at peak boost to challenge that strange, unearthly disc that had appeared again— from somewhere in space . . .

With the throttle-lever jammed forward through the gate, the powerful V-12 engine pounded to peak revs, thrusting its enormous energy to the triple-blade prop and hurling the slim grey *Spitfire* upward against the stars . . . higher . . . higher . . . while Vic Spiers felt the pressure against his spine, the pulsing of the twelve frenzied cylinders through his body, the fierce trembling of the control-column under his gaunt-leted hand.

His eyes raked the instruments in a routine check. Revs: *maximum*. Boost: *maximum*. Rate of climbs: *maximum*. His eyes flicked up to the windshield, satisfied that his machine was pulling him into the night-sky with every sinew at top tension, every component straining at peak strength against gravity. And as his eyes lifted to the windshield's inch-thick laminated glass, they glimpsed the disc . . . his aerial prey . . . the weird aircraft that had appeared over Brinton Field for the second time in three weeks . . . the immense and unearthly form that, for the second time in three weeks, Spiers was chasing into the stars.

His radio voiced,

"We can see it from the ground . . . You're gaining on it! Keep going, Vic!"

He sent no answer. His mouth was dry with excitement and with awe as he watched the huge saucer-shaped form in his camera-gun sights—and now, as if his memory had snatched him back to a world at war, his thumb hit the gun-button . . . again . . . again . . . as the flying disc whirled dead in the sights, a mere 2,000 feet above the climbing *Spitfire*. No shells ripped from his mainplanes, but the camera was operating silently, shooting the disc with its winking, remembering eye.

Then it was that proof came, as it had before, three weeks ago—proof that the disc was no experimental machine run amok—proof that from within its whirling mass a keen intelligence controlled its headlong flight; for now it veered, with a suddenness that caught Vic's breath in his parched throat . . . veered to port and shot downwards, evading the *Spitfire's* implacable pursuit.

Against the backcloth of the night-sky the mad hunt ran on. The disc, now brilliant with banners of streaming blue exhaust-light, shot downwards ahead of the power-diving plane, veered to starboard with a turn of speed that Vic knew could never be resisted by a human body, climbed suddenly as it had climbed before . . . to 15,000 feet . . . 17,000 . . . 19,000 . . . until the dogging *Spitfire* seemed to hang by an invisible thread from that blinding blue miracle that fled against the heavens. 20,000 feet, and the distance between the hunter and the prey was 1,000 . . . 22,000 feet, and the distance closed to 500 . . . 23,000 feet, and suddenly, strangely, the hunter lost speed, swerved in a sickening arc, and began diving, plunging for the dark landscape below.

For an instant the disc hovered, like a tilted moon, then rose, swift as a rocket, and was gone.

Against the deaf ears of the slumped *Spitfire* pilot the radio-call came up from the ground,

"*Vic . . . Vic! What's happened—you seem out of control! Can you hear me, Vic? Over to you, over . . .*"

But from the star-fields the slim grey shape came plummeting to earth; and in the watch-tower of Brinton Field the faces of the signals-crew were white. There came no answer to their frantic call.

A yellow tongue of flame licked suddenly from the instrument panel, where wires were shorting. Vic cut the master-switch and hit the flame with his ribboned gauntlet. Around him was utter silence. His machine had come down in the thick of a wood, and was tilted drunkenly among a nest of saplings. In the few precious moments of returning consciousness he had woken to his peril, and had dragged the column back, flopping the *Spitfire* across the saplings, belly down.

He counted his arms and legs, and found the usual number. His head was still screwed on, and faced the right direction. He gave a grunt of relief.

51

"Fair enough . . ." he said, and climbed out of the cockpit. Clinging to the saplings, he pulled out the miniature Geiger counter that his brother had given him three weeks before. It reacted, as he had guessed it would. The plane was slightly radioactive . . . and that meant one thing: the flying disc was powered by an atomic engine. He stowed the Geiger, and released the camera-gun from its bed, and took it with him to the ground, swinging and clambering down the tangled saplings and ripping half his flying-suit to shreds before his feet hit moss. Then he began walking, out of the starlit wood.

While the prints were drying, Brainstorm Spiers sat his brother down in his snug laboratory-cum-study, and brought in a tray of scalding coffee. Behind his spectacles, his eyes were alive with excitement.

"All right, Vic, as soon as you feel like it—shoot!"

Vic Spiers sat relaxed, his body still sore from the pummelling the crash-landing had given it.

"The story's brief," he said, "but I don't think it'll bore you . . . I chased the disc all over the sky, and then followed it upwards, to beyond 22,000 feet. You can call me a fool— I was one. My oxygen equipment was down on the ground, being checked over. There hadn't been time to put it on board when I took off—I was in too much of a hurry to get airborne after the prey . . ."

"You blacked-out after 22,000 feet?"

Vic nodded. "Yep. And came to when Mother Earth was careering up at me like an express lift. I pancaked on to a spinney and got off with bruises. But that isn't the important thing—"

"Important enough . . ." said Brainstorm, soberly. "I rather like having a crazy brother around."

Vic grinned. "Well, you've still got one, feller." He leaned forward. "But the important thing is that your

Geiger reacted—you've seen the readings. So we know what kind of an engine it uses."

"Atomic."

"Exactly. Has anyone on Earth produced such an engine? It's impossible! Every great scientist has said it'll be ten years—even more—before we can approach that stage of atomic development. And even if we have produced one, so soon, have we made one as big as that? I tell you, Brainstorm, that disc was fifty times as big as the one I chased three weeks ago—even the watch-tower crew saw it, high above me! It must weigh a hundred tons—even if it's made of balsa-wood!"

Brainstorm nodded quietly, sipping his coffee.

"If those photographs develop all right," Vic went on, "I'm taking them to Group-Captain Barnes. That'll convince the man—plus those Geiger readings . . ."

"It should, Vic. It should. You didn't come near to losing your life chasing a flock of birds . . . Any more than Mantell did in 1948."

"Mantell? Who's he?"

"American flyer. He did the same thing as you, over Godman Field, 7th January, three years ago. He radioed his watch-tower that he was chasing a disc that was 'immense' and brightly lit. He neared 20,000 feet—and then his plane simply disintegrated, killing him."

Vic's tone was quiet. "Maybe it was lucky I blacked out," he said. His brother nodded.

"Maybe it was, Vic, or you might have gone Mantell's way." He got up. "Stay where you are, and relax for a while —you need to." He went into the dark-room, but was back in a moment, breathless. Film-print flapped in his hands, still gleaming wet.

"They're not dry yet—but just take a look!"

Together they stared at the pictures under the desk-lamp.

There were three duds, two blurred ones and four perfect shots . . . of a giant twin disc, double-decked, and with rows of portholes round the lower rim. From the slotted ducts on the upper rim, white streamers rushed against the jet-black sky.

Brainstorm's voice was a low gasp.

"So that's what you were hunting . . . suffering cats! Even if those portholes are no bigger than a human head, the thing must be twice the size of the Queen Mary!"

Vic nodded. He was as excited as Brainstorm—but not in the least amazed. He'd watched this Devil Disc through his own windshield, a few hours before. He knew what his *Spitfire* had taken on—a metal Goliath that could never have been built on Earth, that had turned so swiftly in the air that no human body could have withstood the colossal pressure-change. He and his brother were looking at pictures of a ship from another planet. All doubt was gone.

He picked up his driving-gloves, checking his watch.

"I'm taking these prints to Barnes, right away! If he's not at his office, I'll find him somewhere else. Can I have those Geiger readings?"

Brainstorm snatched up his pad.

"Let me drive you, Vic—you still look a bit shaky on your pins. Couple of hours ago you were coming out of the sky like an express train into the trees, remember!"

They reached the door together, and Vic snapped out,

"I know. And that's just how I'm going into that Groupie's office . . . come on, Brainstorm!"

Group-Captain Barnes was not at Air Security H.Q. His secretary gave Spiers a curious look as he said,

"My chief's gone to Brinton Field, Mr Spiers. To check up personally on a smashed *Spitfire* . . . That wouldn't be yours, would it?"

"Who knows?" jerked out Vic, and steered his brother out of the building and back to the car. "Brinton, feller, and get rid of any moss."

The white Allard slipped like a wraith through the gates and turned westwards through the night. In half an hour they were talking to Max Browning in the watch-tower. He told them,

"The Groupie was here a few minutes after you left, and he wanted to see you. I didn't say where you were, because I thought you ought to get those films developed before he pinched the whole outfit."

Vic nodded. He'd told Max about Barnes, when he had looked in here to pick up his Allard after the smash.

"Where is he now?" he asked.

"Looking over your kite, in Booker's Wood."

"Thanks. If we miss him on the way, tell him he can see me if he waits here till I get back! Brainstorm—next stop, Booker's Wood!"

"Where's that?"

"You just put your foot down, and I'll tell you when to bank . . ."

Brainstorm drove well to precise orders. Ten minutes passed beneath the sports car's hungry wheels, and then they got out, parking it by the roadside. Crossing a meadow, they came upon lights winking through the trees. On the scene was a breakdown-tractor and a crash-crew with slings and tackle, ropes and hand-lamps. As the Spiers brothers came through the spinney the stocky figure of Barnes turned from the group.

"So you couldn't leave it alone, Spiers," he greeted them brusquely. Vic shook his head.

"No, sir, it's just too interesting. This is my brother. Brainstorm—Group-Captain Barnes of Air Security." The two men nodded in the light of the hand-lamps. Barnes said,

"I suppose I ought to congratulate you on getting away with your neck."

"You can congratulate me, yes, but on something quite different. I came down bird's-nesting with my *Spit*—but I got what I went up for. Photographs."

Barnes gripped his arm, lowered his voice.

"Is that true, Spiers?"

"As true as the flying disc . . ."

"Then will you come with me—somewhere where we can talk?"

"We'd be glad. My brother is in on this, too. He's a professional astro-physicist."

"Very well. His help will be valuable."

As they turned away, Vic said: "I told those chaps not to monkey with my wreck. It's radioactive."

Then Barnes said an amazing thing.

"Yes, I know. My men discovered that. The crash-gang's using protective clothing."

"Your men discovered it? Then they must have expected it . . . and brought instruments!"

"Correct. But we'll talk about that—in secret."

The Group-Captain closed the door of the little store-room below the watch-tower and turned to face Vic and Brainstorm, pulling out a briar pipe and filling it.

"This little conference", he said, "is going to be less formal than the last one, and more interesting—for you. But first—may I see those photographs?"

Vic turned. His brother produced them. For perhaps two full minutes Barnes studied them; and when he looked up at Vic his hard blue eyes were excited.

"Nice pictures, Mr Spiers. You're quite a cameraman."

"If I'd carried shells instead of film, I might have brought you some bits and pieces instead of pictures."

Barnes shook his head. "No," he said. "You won't bring down one of those spaceships with ordinary bullets. Their armour's too tough." He struck a match for his pipe. Vic stared.

"You—*you* believe it was a spaceship?"

The Group-Captain nodded, blowing out smoke.

"Air Security has believed it for the past three years, so you don't have to waste your time convincing me." He slid his hands into his jacket pockets, eyeing the brothers with his head erect. "Gentlemen, I'm going to talk. Are you going to listen?"

"Shoot," said Vic.

"It is believed beyond doubt that the discs are space-craft sent to observe Earth from some unidentified planet in the Solar System. In fact, some authorities already believe that the discs are manned by intelligent beings—beings far more developed mentally than man, but of the same kind of structure as insects."

Brainstorm released his breath.

"*In*-sects?"

Barnes nodded. "It's very probable—and not very strange, when you work it out. The insect-structure, with no outer flesh or human-like blood system, could withstand the enormous pressure changes that must take place when these discs manoeuvre in space." He shrugged. "But that's by the way. The point is this—of all the evidence so far produced, these photographs of yours are probably the best to date. You are determined—obviously—to find out all you can of the discs. Three weeks ago, my men heard your radio-call going down to this tower. We tap all calls, over a wide network. That is why those two Security Investigators grabbed you so quickly . . . I tried to get you to keep off the discs, for the reasons I gave you that night. But you're too keen."

Vic faced him in silence. Brainstorm thought he knew

what was coming, and maybe was right. Barnes said,

"We want keen men, as observers, photographers, disc-hunters. I've authority to make a proposition to you. Your *Spitfire* is a mess. We'll give you a brand-new jet aircraft instead. We'll give you a battery of camera-guns. We'll give you a genuine—but unofficial—roving commission, with Squadron-Leader's service pay, although you'll remain a civilian. In return—bring us all the evidence, photographs and information you collect."

There was silence in the tiny store-room.

Vic gave a sudden, exuberant grin of joy.

"And a new flying-suit? I got mine shredded."

The Group-Captain smiled.

"And a new flying-suit, Spiers. Fleece-lined."

He held out his hand and Vic grasped it.

"And my brother's assistance, sir?"

Barnes nodded. "If you both keep a vow of secrecy that you're working for Air Security. It might not be long before we can release the news to the world; but when we do we must have clearer evidence than we have now. We hope the intentions of this mysterious planet are not warlike. We don't believe they are—in every case except Captain Thomas Mantell's, these discs have avoided a fight; and we think his death was accidental—he was caught in that gigantic exhaust-blast. As soon as we can tell the public that these visitors deserve our welcome on Earth, then we'll release the news. And you two will help us?"

Brainstorm nodded, his freckled face eager. Vic said with a grin, "Can a disc fly?"

Less than a month after the grey *Spitfire* had plunged across Booker's Wood, a privately-owned Vampire-jet was berthed in the hangars at Brinton Field. It was fitted with four super-fast cameras, buried in the mainplanes and linked with the gun-button in the cockpit.

Day after day, night upon night, its young owner strolled on the tarmac, talked with the tower-crew, sat perched on the edge of a starter-trolley near his machine. Hour by patient hour, with the glow of sundown or the sheen of starlight on his eager face, the Earthling waited . . . for the coming of the ship from—where?

Until, six nights after he had taken command of his new, wickedly fast jet-aircraft, his time came . . . as it had come before. But now he was more prepared.

As the thin flicker of blue light was sighted among the high-drifting clouds, a lamp winked from the alerted watch-tower. Vic Spiers grabbed his helmet.

"*Take-off!*" His yell echoed against the hangars as two mechanics came sprinting to the machine. All was checked and on top-line: fuel, cameras, oxygen, radio. The cockpit-hood slid shut. The starter-contact banged home. The engine, already warm, choked into life and sent its sudden thunder slamming across the field.

From the tower—the green light.

From the cockpit—the pilot's signal.

From the mechanics—the "*all clear! . . .*"

They stood back. The machine trembled, and rolled into movement. Three minutes and fifteen seconds later, it slipped like a dark javelin along the runway and then lifted . . . its metal snout nosing into the free air that was its element.

From Space the disc had come. From Earth, the hunter rose. The chase was on!

Barnstormers

DON DWIGGINS

*Flying Darevevils of the Roaring Twenties is the stirring title of
the book from which this extract is taken. It sums up the almost fanatical
verve with which men—and women—took to the air once flying became a practical possibility and it is astonishing to realize that the
stuntmen and aerial acrobats described here were in many cases already
in their teens when the Wright Brothers made their historic flight at
Kittyhawk or Blériot his epic cross-channel flight.*

"There are old pilots and there are bold pilots, but there are
no old, bold pilots," goes a barnstormer's adage. The same
thing may be said of the "gipsy moths", roving bands of
parachute jumpers who even more than men with wings
surely knew that one mis-step meant sudden death.

Now and then, in some remote airfield hangar, at some
obscure county fair, you'll still find a few living, old-bold
ones, last of the breed of thrill-seekers, men who cheated
death a dozen times, plus a few women dare-devils, also
living on borrowed time.

Around rigging tables at scores of modern skydiving D.Z.'s
(drop zones), you'll still hear gossip about their feats, and
how they did the impossible and lived to tell about it. And
about others who didn't. Much of the lore is legendary; most
stories get better with retelling. But many were true.

There was dynamic Eddie Angel, a brother of the famed barnstorming jungle pilot Jimmy Angel, a World War I Royal Flying Corps hero who joined the gipsy fliers in the 1920s and operated a cow-pasture squadron of death known as *Jimmy Angel's Flying Circus*. After a wild day's antics, the *Flying Angels* lured suckers back to the field at night to witness Eddie's spectacular "Dive of Death"—a free-fall plunge down the sky from 5,000 feet, while holding a pair of big flashlights.

"When I could see the ground," Eddie once explained to me, "it was time to pull the ripcord."

Then there was Bobby Rose, first of the great Hollywood stuntmen, who made women faint by falling backward off the top wing of a *Jenny* aircraft during a plane change. People shrieked in horror as Bobby tumbled down the sky, head over heels, towards certain death. Finally a 400-foot static line jerked open a hidden 'chute and Bobby floated earthwards with cheers in his ears. "I used to plead with Sky-Hi Irvin to invent a ripcord and make my life easier," Bobby once sighed.

Another old-timer, Ed Unger, in 1967 celebrated his ninety-fifth birthday after a lifetime dedicated to barnstorming as a balloonist and parachutist. It was Ed who taught Sky-Hi Irvin to jump, and he still claims to have originated the idea for the manually controlled, back-pack parachute in use today.

Unger, Rose and many another old-time parachute jumper wintered in Venice, California, for two reasons—the weather was salubrious, and there it was that the early newsreel companies shot most of the early aviation thrillers. Few aerial stuntmen of the 1920s bothered with parachutes. They were cumbersome to lug around while clambering over the outside of *Standards* and *Jennies* while a camera-ship flew in close, getting the action on film.

61

Duke Krantz, who originated the standing loop, scoffed at the idea of a "jump sack". After all, centrifugal force held him in place when he stood on the top wing all through a loop! Another barnstormer with disdain for the parachute was Walter Hunter of the Hunter Brothers Flying Circus. At a time when parachute jumps were standard fare at air meets, this team of four Oklahomans drew the biggest crowds by advertising their speciality—a *Thrilling Death Leap from an Airplane WITHOUT a Parachute!* The Hunters, a rugged band of grease-stained gipsy fliers, capped their show by dragging low across the field in front of the grandstand, Albert, Kenneth and John waving from the cockpits of their *Standard* biplane and Walter swinging by his knees from the axle. He'd let go and drop head-first—right into a haystack.

Many a character used to drift into the old Venice Field hangar looking for stunt work during the Depression years. Of these oddballs, the strangest to Sam Greenwald, an *International Newsreel* cameraman, was a full-blooded Cherokee Indian, Chief Whitefeather, who showed up one day in the early 1920s, thick black hair braided down his back, looking for wampum.*

"Half a dozen pilots and cameramen were playing poker in a corner of the hangar when Whitefeather drifted in," Greenwald remembers. "He told us he wanted to hang by his pigtail from an airplane for fifty dollars."

To make sure that he could do it, they interrupted their game long enough to string the Indian up by his hair, which was tied to a rope thrown over a rafter. "We forgot all about him until that night," says Greenwald. "When we finally went back to cut him down, he was pretty mad, but in good shape."

---

*Originally beads used for currency: in other words, money.

The following day Frank Clarke, one of the top Hollywood stunt fliers, took Chief Whitefeather up two thousand feet over town. He swung happily in the wind while Sam shot movies of him from a camera-ship. Clarke had visions of making a fortune by touring the country with Chief White-feather, the stunt to be sponsored by a hair-restorer company.

Whitefeather had other ideas. He wanted to try an even riskier stunt—a cutaway parachute drop with *ten* 'chutes. His idea was to open them one at a time, cutting away each one as it opened, then land with the tenth. Things went well as cameraman Joe Johnson ground away furiously, following him down the sky in another ship. But Whitefeather's sixth 'chute fouled; he plunged into a barley patch and was killed.

There was something quite dashing about carnival jumpers, handsome young fellows with pencil-line mous-taches and a quick eye for pretty girls, heroes who lounged around small airports in white coveralls, white cloth helmets, and white sneakers. From habitually packing a thirty-pound parachute on their backs, they walked with a forward list as if encountering a stiff headwind.

Such a barnstormer was Jimmie Goodwin, a veteran jumper and Hollywood bit player who added to his costume a pair of canvas batman's wings and a cloth stabilizer be-tween his outspread legs to enable him to descend in spirals. Hank Coffin, a flier who used to take Jimmie up to jump altitude, claimed with a straight face that he once glided all the way down from 10,000 feet, over Big Bear Lake to Alhambra Airport, seventy-five miles away! There are probably less than half a dozen batmen left today, and the work isn't steady, but before World War II no flying circus was complete without one.

Cliff Rose, another barnstorming jumper who knows what it's like to fly like a bird, made his first canvas wings at seven-teen, to become the world's youngest professional batman.

When the regular performer didn't show up at a Long Beach air show, Rose bought some sailcloth and rigged up an outfit that looked fine, but he wasn't too sure it would work.

At ten thousand feet over the airport, Rose stepped out of an *Aeronca*, spread his arms and legs and felt a freedom he had never experienced before. He related the story to me this way—"I knew from the sound of the wind that I was diving faster than I ever had before in thirty standard jumps. I gripped the hand-holds on two broomstick arms and pulled up, drawing the canvas taut. I spread my legs apart and there I was—a batman!

"I decided to try a spiral dive. Cautiously, I raised my right arm and dropped my left, then lifted my head, so that I was a sort of human corkscrew. Below me, the earth began to spin like a top. I was flying!

"I tried a loop next. Both arms extended rigidly, I lifted my head and arched my back. I tumbled over backwards with an easy mushing feeling. From the ground, they said I looked sensational!

"I was so busy trying out my wings I almost forgot about my parachute. In alarm, I realized I was so close to the airport I could see the yokels! I yanked hard on the D-ring, too close for comfort. I hit the ground seconds later."

To prove he was really flying and not just falling erratically, Rose added an extra canvas pocket and filled it with red flour, then painted the blue sky with streaks of slashing red.

There is a bad joke about the fellow who bought a parachute and was told by the salesman that he could bring it back and get a refund if it didn't work, but it really happened to Rose.

"I'd organized a jump team billed as the *Cliff Rose Death Angels*, and I was making a long, free fall. I waited almost too long to pull, trying hard to zero in on a forty-foot ground target. As luck had it, the 'chute streamed and failed to blossom. I barely had sky left to hit the emergency 'chute, and while I missed the spot, I lived to take the big twenty-eight footer back to the complaint desk. They cheerfully refunded my money."

Among other famous batmen were Clem Sohn, the first man to use canvas sails for body gliding (and first to be killed doing it); Leo Valentin, France's famed "human bird", who also died a victim of his crazy contraption, and Roy "Red" Grant, who made headlines by sailing above Niagara Falls from the United States to the Canadian side and back, on home-made wings.

Not all barnstorming jumpers were killed by falling. There were other danger zones around small-town airports that took their toll of lives. Gladys Roy, a pretty wing-walker and jumper with nerves of steel, thrilled many an audience with her leaps into the wild blue yonder, which ended with her landing daintily and reaching for her compact. In Youngstown, Ohio, on 15 August 1927, Gladys lost her life—by accidentally walking into a spinning propeller.

Perhaps the world's greatest raconteur and authority on *Americana barnstormiana* is the irrepressible Louis "Speedy" Babbs, a still-active old-boldster who as much as anybody enjoys hangar flying tales "spun from whole cloth for the benefit of younger pilots, especially those who recently soloed."

Speedy will tell you about the twin brothers who in the twenties almost set a cross-country record of twenty hours in a *Jenny*, east coast to west. One brother, in a blaze of publicity, took off from New York in a *Jenny*, after a $5000 prize. On the side of the plane was emblazoned its name: *Soul of Africa*. He waved farewell to the newsreel camera-ship and winged off into the night—landing in a Pennsylvania cow pasture after dark. At dawn, the other brother arrived in Seattle, having taken off in another *Jenny* from a small town fifty miles to the east. Things went well until the award banquet, when newsreels of the departure and arrival were shown to the admiring audience. The last scene showed *Jenny No. 2* setting down at Seattle's municipal airport, the pilot climbing out smiling broadly. Behind him, in large letters on the fuselage, he had painted *Sole of Africa*.

Speedy remembers an Army pilot named Weaver, stationed in the Canal Zone, who had several forced landings over the ocean. Each time he hit, his plane had nosed over. Finally he figured a way to lick the problem—the next time his engine quit he would glide down inverted. When his plane nosed over, there he would be, right side up!

Wild as some of the hangar flying tales were, Speedy heard few that could top his own personal experiences at cow-pasture dedications in the late 1920s and early 1930s. In his career as a stuntman Babbs broke only fifty-six bones, a few at a time, and so he considers himself pretty indestructible. He started out to be a mere pilot, learning to fly in 1925 with Waldo Waterman, a pioneer birdman, but he couldn't raise enough money to buy an airplane. He invested in a $35 parachute instead.

"I helped to dedicate more cow pastures than you can shake a control stick at," says Speedy, "not only doing parachute jumps and wing-walking, but some fancy rope-ladder stunts, hanging from a *Canuck* by my feet and picking up a flag from the ground, and so forth."

His first break came at the dedication of San Bernardino's Tri-City Airport in Southern California on 13th October 1928. "I was supposed to ride the top wing of Bob Crooks's *Curtiss Oriole*, and while upside down in a loop, trickle off, fall free and open my 'chute as close to the ground as possible. It had never been done before."

Perched on the top wing, Speedy's skinny body nevertheless created such drag that Crooks barely got off the ground, flying *beneath* power lines at the edge of the small airport. "I had to duck to miss 'em!" he says.

Climbing finally to 1,700 feet, as high as the plane would go, Crooks dove for speed and mushed up through a loop. At the top Speedy slid off, and when he got low enough to hear the spectators screaming he reached for the ripcord. It wasn't there. It had fouled underneath his chest pack.

"With the same motion I jerked the rip-line on my spare 'chute. It opened with a jerk, broke three shroud lines and split from the centre to the lip, and then I hit the ground. I hit so hard I believe my tracks are still in the centre of that airport!"

Speedy went to the hospital with two crushed vertebrae that left him paralysed for weeks, but when he got out he went right back to the same airport—and opened a school for jumpers.

"I also did more wing-walking, and once my dad was watching me. This lady next to him, says, "That man must be crazy up there! When he gets down I'd like to see what he looks like!" Dad says, "Lady, stick right with me and I'll introduce you. He's my son!"

With his back not fully healed, Speedy decided to forego parachuting for a while and take up something tamer. So he bought a motor cycle and had a big, steel-mesh ball erected at Ocean Park Amusement Pier, next to Venice, where he set up a world record by looping the loop on the motor cycle inside the "Globe of Death" five hundred times in a row.

It was 1932 when Speedy made further headlines with a wild 4th of July pyrotechnic parachute stunt that literally backfired and darned near killed him. And grabbing headlines wasn't easy that week, for big things were happening everywhere—Franklin D. Roosevelt had just won the Democratic Party's nomination for President in Chicago; Amelia Earhart had made a forced landing near Los Angeles; Jimmy

Mattern and Bennie Griffin were off on their round-the-world flight; Jean Harlow and Paul Bern were honeymooning in Hollywood; and Norma Talmadge was suing Joseph Schenck for divorce.

But all this was brushed aside on 5th July when the Santa Monica *Outlook* bannered the story: *HUMAN SKYROCKET SERIOUSLY BURNED!*

Speedy had made a deal with the Venice Pier manager to jump from an airplane at night and set off a bunch of fireworks on his way down. He went from airport to airport, looking for a pilot to take him up, but was turned down cold.

"I found out later that the C.A.A. (Civil Aviation Authority) had threatened to ground any pilot who took me up," he recalls. "Finally I found a guy who would do it—he needed the money to lift a mortgage on his plane."

Speedy's angel of mercy was Chuck Sisto, a barnstormer who later made headlines himself as an airline pilot accidentally, when his trim tabs stuck, doing half an outside loop over Texas with a *DC-4* loaded with terrified passengers.

Sisto flew Speedy up to 8,000 feet over Venice Pier in the early evening and found the pier obscured from view by a 3,000-foot cloud layer. Babbs decided to jump anyway, needing the money, so he crawled out to the wing-tip, waved goodbye to Sisto and did a pull-off.

Hanging from his feet was a 100-pound gunny sack full of star bombs and powerful red, white and blue flares, and a big inner tube for a life preserver. "I thought I'd light a couple of star bombs and see how the fuse was timed for distance," he relates. "The first bomb I lit dropped sparks inside the sack and all hell cut loose. The inner tube caught fire and blew out, and I set it swinging so that it would only burn me as it passed below my feet. The star bombs were blowing up inside the sack and my clothes caught fire. The only way to unload that sack was to reach inside and throw the stuff out—I'd left my jack-knife at the airport.

"Many of the pieces exploded in my hands, and I could smell my own flesh burning. But I had to keep on going—in the bottom of the sack was a large detonating bomb that was to be the finale. I knew that if that bomb exploded while still in the bag it would also blow me into little bitty pieces. How I did it, I'll never know, but I finally got it overboard . . . and you know something? It never did go off!"

The irony of the occasion was that all this action took place high above the cloud layer. Says Speedy, "No one saw it but me. My only regret was that I was the only one who saw that magnificent display!"

Meanwhile, back on the ground, people got tired of waiting and started to go home, which prompted the worried pier manager to call the airport. When Sisto informed him that Speedy had jumped half an hour before, rescue boats hurried out and picked him up, more dead than alive, two miles off shore.

Speedy was amused to read his own obituary in the Los Angeles *Times*, whose report of his death was, as Mark Twain once put it in a similar circumstance, greatly exaggerated.

On 17th December 1933, on the thirtieth anniversary of the Wright Brothers' first flight at Kittyhawk, Speedy dreamed up another spectacular that almost cost him his life—the "Sky-Hook-Pendulum-Cloud-Swing." Speedy threaded three parachutes on to eight hundred feet of rope, one atop the other, with the nebulous idea of doing a pull-off at eight thousand feet and swinging down the sky in giant half-mile arcs while burning smoke-pots, so the folks on the ground could follow him.

For added insurance, he fortunately carried an emergency pack. The thought of landing at the end of a half-mile downswing unnerved even this cool character.

Things started off well. He crawled out on to the wing and clipped the rope to his harness, then released the triple 'chute rig, which finally jerked him into space.

"After falling long enough for the slack to be taken up, nothing happened," he remembers. "I grabbed the rope to relieve the shock on my harness and pulled in a few feet of it. The rope felt strangely slack, so I made a few more overhand grabs and there I was, holding the frayed end! It had broken about twenty feet above me!"

With more than 3,000 feet of the sky already used up, Speedy lived up to his name by grabbing for the D-ring. But a horrible thought flashed across his mind—his life now depended on an old canopy that had been repeatedly immersed in sea-water and hadn't been repacked in months.

"It opened like a charm, though," he says. "To keep my act from being a total flop, I lit the smoke-pots anyway, then spun the 'chute all the way to the ground—right in front of the grandstand, naturally."

Speedy's other 'chutes meanwhile drifted to earth miles away, and before he could locate them, one had been stolen. The next day he tried the stunt again with the two remaining 'chutes and got involved in still another adventure. Due to a stiff ocean breeze, he had decided to jump out over the Pacific Ocean, hoping to be blown back to the airport by the time he reached terra firma, but a lower wind-shift tricked him.

"Through force of habit I put the soles of my shoes together and took a drift sight between them. I was drifting out over the bay, instead of in towards land! I whipped out my sheath-knife, cut loose from the two 'chutes and dropped, keeping my eye on the mountain ridge inland. When I had dropped to a level I was sure was dead air I popped the emergency 'chute. I took another drift sight; I was slowly drifting shore-ward toward the airport, though still too far out over the bay for comfort. But my luck held and I landed within twenty steps of the water's edge."

Eventually Speedy recovered all three 'chutes, but he never again tried the "Sky-Hook-Pendulum-Cloud-Swing."

Another of Speedy's great ideas that didn't work was something he dreamed up and sold to *Paramount News*. ("When I was broke I could always sell *Paramount News* a stunt," he says.)

"First I sold Spud Manning on the idea. We were to go up and jump out of a blimp—and swap parachutes on the way down."

Due to a misunderstanding, the camera-ship thought the blimp was only up for a rehearsal (*nobody* would attempt such a fool stunt without practice!), and so the boys waited up there at 4,000 feet in the big sausage while the camera crew went to lunch.

"Our heavy 'chutes and harnesses got mighty uncomfortable, so we took them off and played a game to kill time . . . see who could lean out of the door furthest. That wasn't too much fun, so we tried hanging by our hands, dangling our bodies in space, until the pilot, turning green, pleaded with us to put our 'chutes back on."

When the photo-ship finally got off the ground, Spud and Speedy jumped together but missed, by a wide margin, coming close enough to trade 'chutes.

Speedy: "The next day I tied a mile-long linen string to my harness and rolled it into a ball, which I threw to Spud as we floated down. He was supposed to reel me in to where we could unbuckle and swap harnesses. But the string broke,"

On the third try Lady Luck was either with them or against them, depending on how you want to look at it, for errant winds kept them from risking their lives in a foolhardy stunt that could have been the death of both of them.

Spud Manning, in fact, was one of Speedy Babbs's four

partners to die in action, drowning in Lake Michigan when his plane ran out of gas during the 1933 World Fair. The first of them to go had been Jimmy Young, who lost a struggle against a windstorm that blew his parachute out to sea. Next was a jumper named Curly Wells, another barnstorming gipsy moth. His last partner, Jimmy Pate, waited too long to pull the ripcord on a delayed drop and left his mark in Natchez, Mississippi.

Incidentally, Jimmy Pate's jump pilot was J. O. "Doc" Dockery, an old-time barnstormer who during World War II ran a cow-pasture operation at a small field near Stuttgart, Arkansas, an advanced Glider Corps training base. Due to the usual sort of wartime foul-up, the A.A.F. had provided 1,600 student glider pilot trainees with only *four CG-4A* boxcar gliders. To keep their hand in, the students used to rent *Piper Cubs* from Doc Dockery and buzz freight trains chugging along the Missouri & Arkansas Railroad tracks. A favourite game, to the discomfort of the engineer, was to try to land on a moving flat car on a straight stretch of track.

One of Speedy's pals who worked for the *Paramount News* thrillers was a carnival escape artist named Joe Campi, who came up with the remarkable idea of having himself nailed inside a box slung under the belly of a *Hisso Jenny* plane. He was supposed to be dropped from 8,000 feet, then pull a release rope that would let the box come apart so he could parachute down.

"Well," says Speedy, "Joe dropped fine, but due to air-resistance, the release jammed. Joe literally kicked that box to pieces and got out just in time."

Another of Speedy's crowd was Bob Coy, whom he calls "the best precision jumper I ever saw drop out of the sky." One time down in Pensacola, Florida, Speedy recalls, "the local television studio asked Bob if he could land on the lawn at the studio and then walk right in for an interview. He said he could and we got him the necessary clearances, but the airport control tower neglected to tell the Navy what we were doing. It was at the time of the Bay of Pigs incident and Fidel Castro was threatening to bomb Florida cities. There were lots of clouds that day, but I found a hole and dropped Bob through it. He opened up and slipped his 'chute to land about fifty feet from the door of the TV studio, right on the sidewalk.

"As he'd planned, Coy rolled up his 'chute, tucked it under his arm, and ran inside, right into the camera lens, for a video-tape that was to be broadcast later that day. By coincidence, somebody with a vivid imagination driving past saw Coy drop out of the sky and run into the studio. He stopped and grabbed a phone and called the Navy base, sure it was a Castro invasion, reasoning that invaders would naturally take over communications first. Well, they scrambled every plane they could, but by that time I had landed. We both caught hell."

If Bob Coy was lucky that time, he was far luckier in the summer of 1967 when he was one of only two survivors rescued from the storm-lashed waters of Lake Erie, following a tragic mass-parachute jump that took fourteen lives. An overcast sky had hidden their watery grave from the jumpers until it was too late in their free fall to alter their fate.

Bale-out

CHARLES A. LINDBERGH

When aircraft were still comparatively unsophisticated, flying the mail was one of their most honoured and important jobs. Many a famous airman, such as Antoine de Saint-Exupéry, started his career as a postal pilot; Charles Lindbergh was another, and it was after that valuable training and experience that he went on to make the first solo crossing of the Atlantic in 1927—eight years after the British pilots Alcock and Brown had made their pioneer flight from Newfoundland to Ireland.

Night already shadows the eastern sky. To my left, low on the horizon, a thin line of cloud is drawing on its evening sheath of black. A moment ago, it was burning red and gold. I look down over the side of my cockpit at the farm lands of central Illinois. Wheat shocks are gone from the fields. Close, parallel lines of the seeder, across a harrowed strip, show where winter planting has begun. A threshing crew on the farm below is quitting work for the day. Several men look up and wave as my mail plane roars overhead. Trees and buildings and stacks of grain stand shadowless in the diffused light of evening. In a few minutes it will be dark, and I'm still south of Peoria.

How quickly the long days of summer passed, when it was daylight all the way to Chicago! It seems only a few weeks ago, that momentous afternoon in April, when we inaugurated the airmail service. As chief pilot of the line, the honour of making the first flight had been mine. There were photographs, city officials, and handshaking all along the route that day. For was it not a milestone in a city's history, this carrying of the mail by air? We pilots, mechanics, postal clerks, and business executives, at St. Louis, Springfield, Peoria, Chicago, all felt we were taking part in an event which pointed the way toward a new and marvellous era.

But after the first day's heavy load, swollen with letters of enthusiasts and collectors, interest declined. Men's minds turned back to routine business; the air mail saves a few hours at most; it's seldom really worth the extra cost per letter. Week after week, we've carried the limp and nearly-empty sacks back and forth with a regularity in which we take great pride. Whether the mail compartment contains ten letters or ten thousand is beside the point. We have faith in the future. Some day, we know, the sacks will fill.

We pilots of the mail have a tradition to establish. The commerce of the air depends on it. Men have already died for that tradition. Every division of the mail routes has its hallowed points of crash where some pilot on a stormy night, or lost and blinded by fog, laid down his life on the altar of his occupation. Every man who flies the mail, senses that altar and, consciously or unconsciously, in his way, worships before it, knowing that his own next flight may end in the sacrifice demanded.

Our contract calls for five round trips each week. It's our mission to land the St. Louis mail in Chicago in time to connect with planes coming in from California, Minnesota, Michigan, and Texas—a time calculated to put letters in New York City for the opening of the eastern business day.

Three of us carry on this service: Philip Love, Thomas Nelson, and I. We've established the best record of all the routes converging at Chicago, with over ninety-nine per cent of our scheduled flights completed. Ploughing through storms, wedging our way beneath low clouds, paying almost no attention to weather forecasts, we've more than once landed our rebuilt army war-planes on Chicago's Maywood Field when other lines cancelled out, when older and perhaps wiser pilots ordered their cargo to be put on a train. During the long days of summer we seldom missed a flight. But now winter is creeping up on us. Nights are lengthening; skies are thickening with haze and storm. We're already landing by floodlight at Chicago. In a few more weeks it will be dark when we glide down on to that narrow strip of cow pasture called the Peoria Airmail Field. Before the winter is past, even the meadow at Springfield will need lights. Today I'm over an hour late—engine trouble at St. Louis.

Lighting an airport is no great problem if you have money to pay for it. With revolving beacons, boundary markers and floodlights, night flying isn't difficult. But our organization can't buy such luxuries. There's barely enough money to keep going from month to month.

The Robertson Aircraft Corporation is paid by the pounds of mail we carry, and often the sacks weigh more than the letters inside. Our operating expenses are incredibly low; but our revenue is lower still. The Corporation couldn't afford to buy new aircraft. All our planes and engines were purchased from Army salvage, and rebuilt in our shops at Lambert Field. We call them *D.H.*'s, because the design originated with De Havilland, in England. They are bi-planes, with a single, twelve-cylinder, 400 hp *Liberty* engine in the nose. They were built during the war for bombing and observation purposes, and improved types were put on production in the United States. The military *D.H.* has two cockpits. In our planes the mail compartment is where the front cockpit used to be, and we mail pilots fly from the position where the wartime observer sat.

We've been unable to buy full night-flying equipment for these planes, to say nothing of lights and beacons for the fields we land on. It was only last week that red and green navigation lights were installed on our *D.H.*'s. Before that we carried nothing but one emergency flare and a pocket flashlight. When the dollars aren't there, you can't draw cheques to pay for equipment. But it's bad economy, in the long run, to operate a mail route without proper lights. That has already cost us one plane. I lost a *D.H.* just over a week ago because I didn't have an extra flare, or wing lights, or a beacon to go back to.

I encountered fog that night, on the northbound flight between Marseilles (Illinois) and Chicago. It was a solid bank, rolling in over the Illinois River valley. I turned back south-west, and tried to drop my single flare so I could land on one of the farm fields below; but when I pulled the release lever nothing happened. Since the top of the fog was less than 1,000 feet high, I decided to climb over it and continue on my route, in the hope of finding a clear spot around the air-mail field. Then, if I could get under the clouds, I could pick up the Chicago beacon, which had been installed at government expense.

Glowing patches of mist showed me where cities lay on the Earth's surface. With these patches as guides, I had little trouble locating the outskirts of Chicago and the general area of Maywood. But a blanket of fog, about 800 feet thick, covered the field. Mechanics told me afterward that they played a searchlight upward and burned two barrels of gasoline on the ground in an effort to attract my attention. I saw no sign of their activities.

After circling for a half-hour, I headed west, hoping to pick up one of the beacons on the transcontinental route. They were fogged in, too. By then I had discovered that the failure of my flare to drop was caused by slack in the release cable, and that the flare might still function if I pulled on the cable instead of on the release lever. I turned south-west, towards the edge of the fog, intending to follow my original plan of landing on some farmer's field by flarelight. At 8.20 p.m. my engine spat a few times and cut out almost completely. At first I thought the carburettor jets had clogged, because there should have been plenty of fuel in my main tank. But I followed the emergency procedure of turning on the reserve. Then, since I was only 1500 feet high, I shoved the flashlight into my pocket and got ready to jump; but power surged into the engine again. Obviously nothing was wrong with the carburettor—the main tank had run dry. That left me with reserve fuel for only twenty minutes of flight—not enough to reach the edge of the fog.

I decided to jump when the reserve tank ran dry, and I had started to climb for altitude when a light appeared on the ground—just a blink, but that meant a break in the fog. I circled down to 1200 feet and pulled out the flare-release cable. This time the flare functioned, but it showed only a solid layer of mist. I waited until the flare sank out of sight on its parachute, and began climbing again. Ahead, I saw the glow from a small city. I banked away, toward open country.

I was 5000 feet high when my engine cut the second time. I unbuckled my safety belt, dived over the right side of the fuselage, and after two or three seconds of fall pulled the ripcord. The parachute opened right away. I was playing my flashlight down toward the top of the fog bank, when I was startled to hear the sound of an airplane in the distance. It was coming toward me. In a few seconds I saw my *D.H.*, dimly, less than a quarter-mile away and about on a level with me. It was circling in my direction, left wing down. Since I thought it was completely out of gasoline, I had neglected to cut the switches before I jumped. When the nose dropped, due to the loss of the weight of my body in the tail, some additional fuel apparently drained forward into the carburettor, sending the plane off on a solo flight of its own.

My concern was out of proportion to the danger. In spite of the sky's tremendous space, it sounded crowded with traffic. I shoved my flashlight into my pocket and caught hold of the parachute-risers so I could slip the canopy one way or the other in case the plane kept pointing toward me. But it was fully a hundred yards away when it passed, leaving me on the outside of its circle. The engine noise receded, and then increased until the *D.H.* appeared again, still at my elevation. The rate of descent of plane and parachute were approximately equal. I counted five spirals, each a little farther away than the last. Then I sank into the fog bank.

Knowing the ground to be less than 1,000 feet below, I reached for the flashlight. It was gone. In my excitement when I saw the plane coming toward me, I hadn't pushed it far enough into my pocket. I held my feet together, guarded my face with my hands, and waited. I heard the *D.H.* pass once again. Then I saw the outline of the ground, braced myself for impact, and hit—in a cornfield. By the time I got back on my feet, the 'chute had collapsed and was lying on top of the corn tassels. I rolled it up, tucked it under my arm, and started walking between two rows of corn. The stalks were higher than my head. The leaves crinkled as I brushed past them. I climbed over a fence, into a stubble field. There I found wagon tracks and followed them. Ground visibility was about 100 yards.

The wagon tracks took me to a farmyard. First, the big barn loomed up in a haze. Then a lighted window beyond it showed that someone was still up. I was heading for the house when I saw an automobile move slowly along the road and stop, playing its spotlight from one side to the other. I

CHARLES A. LINDBERGH

walked over to the car. Several people were in it.

"Did you hear that airplane?" one of them called out as I approached.

"I'm the pilot," I said.

"An airplane just dived into the ground," the man went on, paying no attention to my answer. "Must be right near here. God, it made a racket!" He kept searching with his spotlight, but the beam didn't show much in the haze.

"I'm the pilot," I said again. "I was flying it." My words got through that time. The spotlight stopped moving.

"*You're the pilot?* Good God, how—"

"I jumped with a parachute," I said, showing him the white bundle.

"You aren't hurt?"

"Not a bit. But I've got to find the wreck and get the mail sacks."

"It must be right near by. Get in and we'll drive along the road a piece. Good God, what went wrong? You must have had *some* experience! You're sure you aren't hurt?"

We spent a quarter of an hour searching, unsuccessfully. Then I accompanied the farmer to his house. My plane, he said, had flown over his roof only a few seconds before it struck the ground. I asked to use his telephone. The party line was jammed with voices, all talking about the airplane that had crashed. I broke in with the statement that I was the pilot, and asked the telephone operator to put in emergency calls for St. Louis and Chicago. Then I asked her if anyone had reported the exact location of the wreck. A number of people had heard the plane pass overhead just before it hit, she replied, but nothing more definite had come in.

I'd hardly hung up and turned away when the bell rang—three longs and a short.

"That's our signal," the farmer said.

Bale-out

My plane had been located, the operator told me, about two miles from the house I was in. We drove to the site of the crash. The *D.H.* was wound up in a ball-shaped mass. It had narrowly missed a farmhouse, hooked one wing on a grain shock a quarter of a mile beyond, skidded along the ground for eighty yards, ripped through a fence, and come to rest on the edge of a cornfield. Splinters of wood and bits of torn fabric were strewn all around. The mail compartment was broken open and one sack had been thrown out, but the mail was undamaged—I took it to the nearest post office to be entrained.

F

Earthworm's First Flight

F. YEATS-BROWN

Flying in the World War I was already far developed. By 1917, German aircraft were bombing London—far more effectively than the Zeppelins that had preceded them. By 1918, the great Handley-Page night bombers were operational, carrying six 112-pound bombs each. Here, from his Bengal Lancer, Yeats-Brown tells of his first flight as an observer over the Syrian desert, after he had wangled his way into the Royal Flying Corps without having any previous experience.

This is the morning of my first flight. Dust devils are swirling through the date-palms. The wind lifts sheets of sand off the Arab graveyard bordering the aerodrome, and the temperature is well over 100 degrees Fahrenheit in the shade.

Start the "prop"? Certainly!

"Look out! You'll get your head chopped off!"

Stupid! I was trying to swing the propeller while standing underneath it. Here's a mechanic to help. I'll watch the way he does it.

"Contact!" A heave and splutter of the engine. "Contact!" The *Maurice Farman* is popping on most of her valves, slowly, fast, faster, now with a roar that rattles my teeth as I climb into the observer's seat behind the pilot. What's this strap for? To tie round me? Well, we're off. Rumpety-bump. The ground slips away.

We've left. We're sailing over the twisting Tigris. There's

a cloud of yellow dust behind us. The leaves of my notebook are trying to tear themselves out in the wind.

Basra looks cool and beautiful amongst its green groves. A filthy hole it is on foot, but here the world is different. There are the marshes of Shaiba, where a battle has been fought; and up there, to the left of the river, near the old Garden of Eden, is the place where, as I was encouragingly told on arriving at the station, two of us had their throats cut by Arabs, the other day, when making a forced landing.

Revs, props, glides, pancakes, pockets, landing T's, *Longhorns*, *Shorthorns*, *Gnomes*, *Le Rhones*—all this talk is not impossible to learn by careful attention to its context. No one knows that I have never flown, and that until yesterday I had not the foggiest idea about even the theory of artillery observation from the air. It is really quite simple, however. I am to fire red, blue and white Very lights to indicate "short", "over" and "range". The battery has strips of cloth to indicate the direction of the target, and the orders of its commander: thus L means "observe for line", X "observe for range", E "repeat last signal".

Also I have made a list of everything required for the equipment of a dark-room. I have tested the *Goerz Graflex* camera (I had used a *Brownie* for years, I comforted myself...).

I have learned the strength of Turkish battalions, brigades, divisions. I have been instructed in how to allow for mirages, count camels, distinguish between Arab and regular cavalry, calculate distances from gun-flash. Soldiering is far more interesting than I thought.

There's a cold wind blowing up my shorts. We have left the layer of hot lead that weighs on Basra. It's glorious up here. Has man ever known such bliss? "To fly in the air is nothing wonderful," my guru said, "for even the dirtiest flies can do it." He was wrong. The world has found a new Yoga and will need new bodies before it can fulfil the possibilities of its last and greatest triumph.

Where's my Very pistol? It's hard to find anything in this gale. The battery has just fired. That salvo fell short. Here's the pistol. A red cartridge. Simple. Now a white, for they have the range. Ouch! That was a bump, I suppose. I'll tell the pilot to circle to the right, towards the Persian frontier, to see if he really does what I tell him.

Take O to R, I scribble in my notebook, and leaning forward, show it to him.

He nods, and banks round so giddily that my inside jumps like a shot black-buck.

I am an observer. Ten minutes ago I was an ignorant earthworm, but as Masefield says, "Life's an affair of instants, spun to years." I am lord now of another dimension; the air is my hope and my love.

Damn! The battery fired again, while I was writing to the pilot, and now we've swung round so that I can't see the result. What is the signal for "not observed"? . . . . Best do nothing.

The battery has now laid out an F on the ground—not "fool", but "fresh target". Their shots have gone over: a blue light. Now short: a red light. Now short again: another red light. Now over: a blue light. I've ripped a fingernail on this foul pistol. They have the range: a white light.

My pilot is scribbling in his notebook.

Lots of oil on our tail, he passes back.

Is there? What happens if you put oil on a Longhorn's tail?

The pilot points downwards. I shrug my shoulders; he shrugs his; in this heat our engines are as temperamental as *prima donnas*. Yes, we may as well land before anything goes wrong. In fact, the quicker the better, for, being an observer, I want to remain one until the next battle.

As long as we don't land among any hostile Arabs . . .

Some Were Unlucky

GUY GIBSON V.C., D.S.O., D.F.C.

The "Dambusters" episode was probably one of the best known and most read of all World War II air stories. It was certainly one of the bravest. The Mohne and Eder dams were vital to the German industrial complex of the Ruhr and the attack, including the invention of a special mine which had to be dropped from a height of only sixty feet, was masterminded by the scientist Barnes Wallis, while the mission itself was led by Wing-Commander Gibson. He was killed in action in 1944.

As we flew over the hill, we saw the Möhne Lake. Then we saw the dam itself. In that light it looked squat and heavy and unconquerable; it looked grey and solid in the moonlight, as though it were part of the countryside itself and just as immovable. A structure like a battleship was showering out flak all along its length, but some came from the powerhouse below it and nearby. There were no searchlights. It was light flak, mostly green, yellow and red, and the colours of the tracer reflected upon the face of the water in the lake. The reflection upon the dead calm of the black water made it seem there was twice as much as there really was.

"Did you say these gunners were out of practice?" asked Spam sarcastically.

"They certainly seem awake now," said Terry.

They were awake all right. No matter what people say, the

Germans certainly have a good warning system. I scowled to myself as I remembered telling the boys an hour or so ago that they would probably only be the Germans' equivalent of the Home Guard and in bed by the time we arrived.

It was hard to say exactly how many guns there were, but tracers seemed to be coming from about five positions, probably making twelve guns in all. It was hard at first to tell the calibre of the shells, but after one of the boys had been hit, we were informed over the R.T. that they were either 20-millimetre type or 37-millimetre, which, as everyone knows, are nasty little things.

We circled around stealthily, picking up the various landmarks upon which we had planned our method of attack, making use of some and avoiding others; every time we came within range of those bloody-minded flak-gunners, they let us have it.

"Bit aggressive, aren't they?" said Trevor.

"Too right they are."

I said to Terry, "God, this light flak gives me the creeps."

"Me too," someone answered.

For a time there was a general bind on the subject of light flak, and the only man who didn't say anything was Hutch, because he could not see it and because he never said anything about flak, anyway. But this was not the time for talking. I called up each member of our formation and found, to my relief, that they had all arrived, except, of course, Bill Astell.* Away to the south, Joe McCarthy had just begun his diversionary attack on the Sorpe. But not all of them had been able to get there; both Byers and Barlow had been shot down by light flak after crossing the coast; these had been replaced by other aircraft of the rear formation. Bad luck, this being shot down after crossing the coast,

*Shot down on the way out.

because it could have happened to anybody. They must have been a mile or so off track and had got the hammer. This is the way things are in flying; you are either lucky or you aren't. We, too, had crossed the coast at the wrong place and had got away with it. We were lucky.

Down below, the Möhne Lake was silent and black and deep, and I spoke to my crew.

"Well, boys, I suppose we had better start the ball rolling." (This with no enthusiasm whatsoever.) "Hello, all *Cooler* aircraft. I am going to attack. Stand by to come into attack in your order when I tell you."

Then to Hoppy: "Hello, 'M-Mother'. Stand by to take over if anything happens."

Hoppy's clear and casual voice came back—"O.K., Leader. Good luck."

Then the boys dispersed to the pre-arranged hiding-spots in the hills, so that they should not be seen either from the ground or from the air, and we began to get into position for our approach. We circled wide and came around down moon, over the high hills at the eastern end of the lake. On straightening up we began to dive towards the flat, ominous water two miles away. Over the front turret was the dam, silhouetted against the haze of the Ruhr Valley. We could see the towers. We could see the sluices. We could see everything. Spam, the bomb-aimer, said, "Good show. This is wizard." He had been a bit worried, as all bomb-aimers are in case they cannot see their aiming points, but as we came in over the tall fir trees his voice came up again rather quickly. "You're going to hit them. You're going to hit those trees."

"That's all right, Spam. I'm just getting my height."

To Terry, "Check height, Terry."

To Pulford, "Speed control, Flight Engineer."

To Trevor, "All guns ready, gunners."

To Spam, "Coming up, Spam."

Terry turned on the spotlights and began giving directions —"Down—down—down. Steady—steady." We were then exactly sixty feet.

Pulford began working the speed; first he put on a little flap to slow us down, then he opened the throttles to get the air-speed indicator exactly against the red mark. Spam began lining up his sights against the towers. He had turned the fusing switch to the *ON* position. I began flying.

The gunners had seen us coming. They could see us coming with our spotlights on from over two miles away. Now they opened up and their tracers began swirling towards us; some were even bouncing off the smooth surface of the lake. This was a horrible moment: we were being dragged along at four miles a minute, almost against our will, towards the things we were going to destroy. I think at that moment the boys did not want to go. I know I did not want to go. I thought to myself, "In another minute we shall all be dead—so what?" I thought again, "This is terrible—this feeling of fear—if it is fear." By now we were a few hundred yards away, and I said quickly to Pulford, under my breath, "Better leave the throttles open now and stand by to pull me out of the seat if I get hit." As I glanced at him I thought he looked a little glum on hearing this.

The *Lancaster* was really moving and I began looking through the special sight on my windscreen. Spam had his eyes glued to the bomb-sight in front, his hand on his button; a special mechanism on board had already begun to work so that the mine would drop (we hoped) in the right spot. Terry was still checking the height. Joe and Trev began to raise their guns. The flak could see us quite clearly now. It was not exactly inferno. I have been through far worse flak fire than that, but we were very low. There was something sinister and slightly unnerving about the whole operation. My aircraft was so small and the dam so large; it was thick and solid, and now it was angry. My aircraft was very small. We skimmed along the surface of the lake, and as we went my gunner was firing into the defences, and the defences were firing back with vigour, their shells whistling past us. For some reason, we were not being hit.

Spam said, "Left—little more left—steady—steady—steady—coming up." Of the next few seconds I remember only a series of kaleidoscopic incidents—

The chatter from Joe's front guns pushing out tracers which bounced off the left-hand flak-tower.

Pulford crouching beside me.

The smell of burnt cordite.

The cold sweat underneath my oxygen mask.

The tracers flashing past the windows—they all seemed the same colour now—and the inaccuracy of the gun positions near the power-station; they were firing in the wrong direction.

The closeness of the dam-wall.

Spam's exultant, "Mine gone."

Hutch's red Very lights to blind the flak-gunners.

The speed of the whole thing.

Someone saying over the R.T., "Good show, leader. Nice work."

Then it was all over, and at last we were out of range, and there came over us all, I think, an immense feeling of relief and confidence.

Trevor said, "I will get those bastards," and he began to spray the dam with bullets until at last he, too, was out of range. As we circled round we could see a great 1,000-feet column of whiteness still hanging in the air where our mine had exploded. We could see with satisfaction that Spam had been good, and it had gone off in the right position. Then, as we came closer, we could that the explosion of the mine had caused a great disturbance upon the surface of the lake and the water had become broken and furious, as though it were being lashed by a gale. At first we thought that the dam itself had broken, because great sheets of water were slopping over the top of the wall like a gigantic basin. This caused some delay, because our mines could only be dropped in calm water, and we would have to wait until all became still again.

We waited.

We waited about ten minutes, but it seemed hours to us. It must have seemed even longer to Hoppy, who was the next to attack. Meanwhile, all the fighters had now collected over our target. They knew our game by now, but we were flying too low for them; they could not see us and there were no attacks.

At last—"Hello, 'M-Mother'. You may attack now. Good luck."

"O.K. Attacking."

Hoppy, the Englishman, casual, but very efficient, keen now on only one thing, which was war. He began his attack.

He began going down over the trees where I had gone from a few moments before. We could see his spotlights quite clearly, slowly closing together as he ran across the water. We saw him approach. The flak, by now, had got an idea from which direction the attack was coming, and they let him have it. When he was about 100 yards away someone said, hoarsely, over the R.T., "Hell! he has been hit."

"M-Mother" was on fire; an unlucky shot had got him in one of the inboard petrol tanks and a long jet of flame was beginning to stream out. I saw him drop his mine, but his bomb-aimer must have been wounded, because it fell straight on to the power-house on the other side of the dam. But Hoppy staggered on, trying to gain altitude so that his crew could bale out. When he had got up to about 500 feet there was a livid flash in the sky and one wing fell off; his aircraft disintegrated and fell to the ground in cascading, flaming fragments. There it began to burn quite gently and rather sinisterly in a field some three miles beyond the dam.

Someone said, "Poor old Hoppy!"

Another said, "We'll get those bastards for this."

A furious rage surged up inside my own crew, and Trevor said, "Let's go in and murder those gunners." As he spoke, Hoppy's mine went up. It went up behind the power-house with a tremendous yellow explosion and left in the air a great ball of black smoke; again there was a long wait while we watched for this to clear. There was so little wind that it took a long time.

Many minutes later I told Mickey to attack. He seemed quite confident, and we ran in beside him and a little in front; as we turned, Trevor did his best to get those gunners, as he had promised.

Bob Hay, Mickey's bomb-aimer, did a good job, and his mine dropped in exactly the right place. There was again a gigantic explosion as the whole surface of the lake shook, then spewed forth its cascade of white water. Mickey was all right; he got through. But he had been hit several times and one wing-tank lost all its petrol. I could see the vicious tracer from his rear-gunner giving one gun position a hail of bullets as he swept over.

Then he called up, "O.K. Attack completed."

It was then that I thought that the dam-wall had moved. Of course we could not see anything, but if Jeff's theory had been correct, it should have cracked by now. If only we could go on pushing it by dropping more successful mines, it would surely move back on its axis and collapse.

Once again we watched for the water to calm down. Then in came Melvyn Young in "D-Dog". I yelled to him, "Be careful of the flak. It's pretty hot."

91

He said, "O.K."

I yelled again, "Trevor's going to beat them up on the other side. He'll take most of it off you."

Melvyn's voice again. "O.K. Thanks." And so as "D-Dog" ran in we stayed at a fairly safe distance on the other side, firing with all guns at the defences, and the defences, like the stooges they were, firing back at us. We were both out of range of each other, but the ruse seemed to work, and we flicked on our identification lights to let them see us even more clearly. Melvyn's mine went in, again in exactly the right spot, and this time a colossal wall of water swept right over the dam and kept on going.

Melvyn said, "I think I've done it. I've broken it."

But we were in a better position to see than he, and it had not rolled down yet. We were all getting pretty excited by now, and I screamed like a schoolboy over the R.T., "Wizard show, Melvyn. I think it'll go on the next one."

Now we had been over the Möhne for quite a long time, and all the while I had been in contact with Scampton Base. We were in close contact with the Air Officer Commanding and the Commander-in-Chief of Bomber Command, and with the scientist, observing his own greatest scientific experiment in Damology. He was sitting in the operations room, his head in his hands, listening to the reports as, one after another, the aircraft attacked. On the other side of the room the Commander-in-Chief paced up and down. In a way their job of waiting was worse than mine. The only difference was that they did not know that the structure was shifting as I knew, even though I could not see anything clearly.

When at last the water had all subsided I called up No. 5—David Maltby—and told him to attack. He came in fast, and I saw his mine fall within feet of the right spot; once again the flak, the explosion and the wall of water. But this time we were on the wrong side of the wall and could not see what had happened. We watched for about five minutes, and it was rather hard to see anything, for by now the air was full of spray. Time was getting short, so I called up Dave Shannon and told him to come in.

As he turned I got close to the dam-wall and then saw what had happened. It had rolled over, but I could not believe my eyes. I heard someone shout, "I think she has gone! I think she has gone!" Other voices took up the cry and quickly I said, "Stand by until I make a recce." I remembered that Dave was going into attack and told him to turn away and not to approach the target. We had a closer look. Now there was no doubt about it; there was a great breach 100 yards across, and the water, looking like stirred porridge in the moonlight, was gushing out and rolling into the Ruhr Valley towards the industrial centres of Germany's Third Reich.

Nearly all the flak had now stopped, and the other boys came down from the hills to have a closer look to see what had been done. There was no doubt about it at all—the Möhne Dam had been breached and the gunners on top of the dam, except for one man, had all run for their lives towards the safety of solid ground; this remaining gunner was a brave man, but one of the boys quickly extinguished his flak with a burst of well-aimed tracer. Now it was all quiet, except for the roar of the water which steamed and hissed its way from its 150-head. Then we began to shout and scream and act like madmen over the R.T., for this was a tremendous sight, a sight which probably no man will ever see again.

Quickly I told Hutch to tap out the message, *Nigger*, to my station, and when this was handed to the Air Officer Commanding there was (I heard afterwards) great excitement in the operations room. The scientist jumped up and danced round the room.

Then I looked again at the dam and at the water, while all around me the boys were doing the same. It was the most amazing sight. The whole valley was beginning to fill with fog from the steam of the gushing water, and down in the foggy valley we saw cars speeding along the roads in front of this great wave of water, which was chasing them and going faster than they could ever hope to go. I saw their headlights burning and I saw water overtake them, wave by wave, and then the colour of the headlights underneath the water changing from light blue to green, from green to dark purple, until there was no longer anything except the water bouncing down in great waves. The floods raced on, carrying with them as they went viaducts, railways, bridges and everything that stood in their path. Three miles beyond the dam the remains of Hoppy's aircraft were still burning gently, a dull red glow on the ground. Hoppy had been avenged.

Moonshot Number One

JULES VERNE

No anthology of the air would be complete without an example of Jules Verne's soaring imagination. There are innumerable fantasies about flight in general, but his astonishing vision of the shape of things to come proved to be an accurate prophecy and Wernher von Braun, doyen of space travel, has acknowledged the debt of modern scientists, for Verne's imaginative stimulus culminated in the actual moon landings of this century. Yet Verne was born only seven years after Napoleon's death.

It was 22nd November. The great departure was to take place ten days later. Only one operation remained to be carried out, a delicate, dangerous operation which required infinite precautions, and against whose success Captain Nicholl had made another bet: the operation of loading the *Columbiad*, of putting the 400,000 pounds of gun-cotton into it. Nicholl had thought, not without reason perhaps, that the handling of such an awe-inspiring quantity of gun-cotton would result in a catastrophe, or at any rate that the highly · explosive mass would ignite under the pressure of the projectile.

The serious dangers involved were increased still further by the nonchalance and frivolity of the Americans who, during the recent Civil War, did not hesitate to load their bombshells with cigars in their mouths. But Barbicane was determined that his experiment should not fail at the last moment; he therefore chose his best workers, watched them at their work, never taking his eyes off them and, by dint of prudent precautions, was able to put the chances of success in his favour.

First of all, he was careful not to bring the whole charge into the Stone Hill enclosure at once. He had brought it in little by little in sealed wagons. The 400,000 pounds of gun-cotton had been divided into 500-pound portions and placed in 800 bulky cartridge bags made with great care by the best craftsmen in Pensacola. The wagons held ten bags each. They came in one by one on the railway from Tampa. In this way, there was never more than 5,000 pounds of gun-cotton within the enclosure at any given time. As soon as each wagon arrived, it was unloaded by barefoot workers and each cartridge bag was taken to the *Columbiad* and lowered into it by means of hand cranes. All steam machinery had been removed from the vicinity, and even the smallest fires had been put out for two miles around. Merely protecting these masses of gun-cotton from the heat of the sun, even in November, was a major undertaking. The work was, therefore, done at night whenever possible, with the aid of a *Ruhmkorff* apparatus which cast a bright, artificial light all the way to the bottom of the *Columbiad*. There the cartridge bags were stacked with perfect regularity and linked by wires which were to carry an electric spark to the centre of each one of them simultaneously.

It was, in fact, by means of a battery that this mass of gun-cotton was going to be ignited. All the wires, surrounded by an insulating material, were united into a single cable near a narrow opening at the height at which the projectile was to be placed; there it passed through the thick cast-iron wall and went up to the surface through a hole in the stone revetment which had been made for that purpose. When it reached the top of Stone Hill the cable continued for a distance of two miles, supported by poles, until it reached a powerful Bunsen battery, after passing through a switch. It would, therefore, only be necessary to push the button of the switch to make the current flow instantaneously and ignite the 400,000 pounds of gun-cotton. Needless to say, the battery was not to be activated until the last moment.

By 28th November the 800 cartridge bags were stacked at the bottom of the *Columbiad*. This part of the operation had been successful. But what worries, anxieties and struggles President Barbicane had been through! He had vainly tried to keep visitors away from Stone Hill; every day people had climbed over the stockade, and some of them had carried rashness to the point of madness by smoking in the midst of the bags of gun-cotton. Barbicane had flown into a rage every day. J. T. Maston had helped as best he could, driving away intruders with great vigour and picking up the burning cigar butts they had tossed here and there. It was a difficult task, for there were more than 300,000 people crowded around the enclosure.

However, since there is a god who looks after artillerymen, nothing blew up and the loading operation was completed. Captain Nicholl was in serious danger of losing his bet, although the projectile had still to be placed in the *Columbiad* and lowered on to the thick layer of gun-cotton.

But before beginning that operation, the objects necessary for the journey were methodically stowed in the projectile. There were quite a few of them, and if Michel Ardan had been allowed to have his way they would soon have taken up all the space reserved for the passengers. It was quite incredible how many things that charming Frenchman wanted to take to the moon—a whole cargo of useless trifles. But Barbicane intervened and the list of objects was reduced to what was strictly necessary. Several thermometers, barometers and telescopes were placed in the instrument chest.

The passengers were eager to examine the moon during the journey; and to facilitate their scrutiny of that new world they decided to take with them Beer and Mädler's excellent map, the *Mappa Selenographica*, printed in four plates and rightly regarded as a masterpiece of observation and patience. It reproduced with scrupulous accuracy the smallest details of that portion of the moon which is turned towards the Earth; mountains, valleys, basins, craters, peaks and rilles were shown with their exact dimensions, correct locations and proper names, from Mount Doerfel and Mount Leibniz, whose tall peak stands in the eastern part of the visible disc, to the *Mare frigoris*, which lies in the northern circumpolar region. It was a valuable document for the travellers, because they could study the new land before ever they set foot on it.

They also took three shotguns and three repeating rifles which fired explosive bullets, plus a very large quantity of powder and shot.

"We don't know whom we may run into," said Michel Ardan. "There may be men or animals who won't take kindly to our coming to pay them a visit. So we must take precautions."

These defensive weapons were accompanied by picks, mattocks, handsaws and other indispensable tools, not to mention clothes suitable for all temperatures, from the cold of the polar regions to the heat of the torrid zone.

Michel Ardan would have liked to take along on his expedition a certain number of animals, though not a couple of every species, for he saw no need to stock the moon with snakes, tigers, alligators and other harmful beasts.

"No," he said to Barbicane, "but a few beasts of burden, such as oxen, cows, donkeys or horses, would look good in the landscape and be very useful to us."

"I agree, my dear Ardan," replied the president of the Gun Club, "but our projectile isn't Noah's Ark; it has neither the same capacity nor the same destination. So let's stay within the limits of the possible."

Finally it was agreed that the travellers would content themselves with taking along an excellent hunting bitch belonging to Nicholl and a prodigiously strong Newfoundland dog. Several boxes of useful seeds were counted among the essential objects. If Michel Ardan had had his way, he would also have taken a few bags of soil to sow them in. He did, in fact, take a dozen shrubs, which were carefully wrapped in a straw covering and placed in a corner of the projectile.

There remained the important question of food, for they had to take into account the possibility that they would land on an absolutely barren portion of the moon. Barbicane managed to pack a year's supply. This is not surprising when one considers that this food consisted of canned meat and vegetables reduced to their minimum volume by a hydraulic press, and that they contained a large amount of nutritive elements. There was not much variety in them, but one could not be particular on such an expedition. There were also fifty gallons of brandy, and a stock of water, though only enough for two months, for as a result of the astronomers' latest observations, no one had any doubt that there was a certain amount of water on the moon. As for food, it would have been ridiculous to believe that inhabitants of the Earth would not find anything to eat up there. Michel Ardan did not have the slightest doubt on the subject. If he had had any doubt, he would not have decided to make the journey.

"Besides," he said one day to his friends, "we won't be completely abandoned by our comrades on Earth, and they'll take care not to forget us."

"Certainly not!" said J. T. Maston.

"What do you mean?" asked Nicholl.

"It's quite simple," replied Ardan. "The *Columbiad* will still be here, won't it? Well, each time the moon is in a favourable position as regards zenith, if not perigee, which will be about once a year, can't our friends send us a shell full of food, which we'll expect on a certain day?"

"Hurrah!" cried J. T. Maston in the tone of a man who had just hit on an idea of his own. "Well said! No, my good friends, we won't forget you!"

"I'm sure you won't. So, you see, we'll have regular news from the Earth, and we, for our part, will be terribly inept if we don't find some way of communicating with our good friends down here!"

These words were spoken with such confidence that Michel Ardan, with his air of determination and his superb self-assurance, could have persuaded the whole Gun Club to come with him. What he said seemed simple, elementary, easy and sure to succeed, and a man would have had to have a truly sordid attachment to this wretched terrestrial globe not to accompany the three travellers on their lunar expedition.

When the various objects had been stowed in the projectile, the water intended to act as a shock-absorber was poured between the partitions and the gas for lighting purposes was compressed into its container. As for the potassium chlorate and the caustic potash, Barbicane, fearing unexpected delays on the way, took enough to replenish the oxygen and absorb the carbonic acid for two months. An extremely ingenious automatic apparatus was installed to purify the air completely and restore its life-giving properties. The projectile was now ready, and all that remained to be done was to lower it into the *Columbiad*—though this was going to be an operation filled with difficulties and perils.

The enormous shell was brought to the top of Stone Hill,

where powerful cranes seized it and held it suspended above the metal pit-shaft.

This was a tense moment. If the chains had broken under the immense weight, the fall of such a mass would undoubtedly have made the gun-cotton explode.

Fortunately this did not happen, and a few hours later the projectile coach, having been slowly lowered down the bore of the cannon, was resting on its explosive eiderdown of gun-cotton. Its weight had no other effect than to compress the charge of the *Columbiad* more tightly.

"I've lost my bet," said the Captain, handing Barbicane $3,000. Barbicane did not want to take this money from his travelling-companion, but he had to yield to Nicholl's insistence; the Captain wanted to fulfil all his obligations before leaving the Earth.

"Then I can only wish you one thing, Captain," said Michel Ardan. "That you'll lose your other bets! If you do, we'll be certain of getting to the moon!"

The first day of December had arrived. It was a fateful day, for if the projectile was not fired that evening at forty-six minutes and forty seconds past ten, more than eighteen years would go by before the moon was in the same simultaneous conditions of zenith and perigee.

The weather was magnificent. In spite of the approach of winter, the sun was shining brightly and bathing in its radiance that globe which was about to lose three of its inhabitants to another world.

How many people slept badly during the night which preceded this impatiently desired day! How many breasts were oppressed by the heavy burden of waiting! All hearts were palpitating with anxiety, except Michel Ardan's. That imperturbable individual came and went with his accustomed air of bustle, but without showing any sign of unusual concern. He had slept peacefully, like Marshal Turenne sleeping on a gun-carriage before battle.

Since dawn a vast crowd had covered the plains which extended around Stone Hill as far as the eye could see. Every quarter of an hour the railway from Tampa brought along more sightseers. This immigration soon assumed fantastic proportions, and according to the *Tampa Observer*, five million people trod the soil of Florida on that memorable day.

For a month the greater part of that crowd had been camping around the enclosure and laying the foundations of a town which has since come to be known as Ardansville. The plain was bristling with huts, cabins and shantics, and these ephemeral dwellings housed a population large enough to arouse the envy of the biggest cities in Europe.

Every nation on earth was represented there; all the languages in the world were spoken at once, in a medley of tongues which recalled the biblical times of the Tower of Babel. The various classes of American society mingled in absolute equality. Bankers, farmers, sailors, buyers, brokers, cotton planters, merchants, boatmen and magistrates rubbed elbows with primitive unceremoniousness. Louisiana creoles fraternized with Indiana farmers, gentlemen from Kentucky or Tennessee and elegant, haughty Virginians chatted with half-wild trappers from the Great Lakes and cattle merchants from Cincinnati. Wearing broad-brimmed white beaver hats or traditional panamas, trousers made of blue cotton from the factories at Opelousas, elegant, unbleached, linen jackets and brightly-coloured boots, they exhibited flamboyant batiste jabots, and on their shirts, cuffs, ties and fingers, and even in their ears, glittered a wide assortment of rings, pins, diamonds, chains, ear-rings and trinkets whose costliness was equalled only by their bad taste. Women, children and servants, dressed with equal opulence, accompanied, followed, preceded and surrounded these husbands, fathers and masters who were like tribal chieftains in the midst of their enormous families.

Such was the vast multitude that waited there hour after hour. Until the evening, a quiet agitation, of the sort which precedes great catastrophes, ran through that anxious crowd. Every mind was in the grip of an ineffable uneasiness, a painful torpor, an indefinable feeling which clutched the heart. Everybody wished it were already over.

However, at about seven o'clock, this heavy silence was suddenly dissipated. The moon rose above the horizon. Several million hurrahs greeted its appearance. It had kept its appointment. Cheers rose up to the heavens and applause broke out on all sides while fair Phoebe shone peacefully in a beautiful sky and caressed that intoxicated crowd with her most affectionate beams.

Just then the three intrepid travellers appeared, and the cheering grew even louder. Unanimously, instantaneously, the American national anthem burst from every panting breast; and *Yankee Doodle*, sung by a chorus of five million voices, rose like a tempest of sound to the uppermost bounds of the atmosphere.

Then, after that irresistible surge of feeling, the anthem died away, the last voices gradually fell silent, the noises faded and a quiet murmur floated above the deeply-moved crowd. Meanwhile, the Frenchman and the two Americans had entered the enclosure around which the crowd was pressing. They were accompanied by the members of the Gun Club and the delegation from the European observatories. Barbicane, cool and calm, quietly gave his final orders. Nicholl, his lips pressed tightly together and his hands behind his back, walked with firm, measured steps. Michel Ardan, as nonchalant as ever, dressed like a typical traveller, with leather gaiters on his feet, a game-bag slung over his shoulder, his brown velvet clothes hanging loosely from his body and a cigar between his teeth, was distributing warm handshakes with princely prodigality as he walked along. His gaiety and verve were irrepressible; he laughed, joked, and played childish tricks on the dignified J. T. Maston; in short, he was French, and even worse, Parisian, to the very end.

Ten o'clock struck. The time had come for the travellers to take their places in the projectile. It would take a certain amount of time to lower them into it, screw down the door-plates, and remove the cranes and scaffolding from the mouth of the *Columbiad*.

The engineer, Murchison, who was going to ignite the gun-cotton by means of an electric spark, had synchronized his chronometer to within a tenth of a second of Barbicane's. The travellers enclosed in the projectile would thus be able to watch the impassive moving hand which would mark the instant of their departure.

The time for farewells had come. It was a touching scene. In spite of his feverish gaiety, Michel Ardan felt moved. J. T. Maston had found under his dry lids an old tear which he had probably been keeping for this occasion. He shed it on the forehead of his dear and worthy president.

"Why don't I come with you?" he said. "There's still time!"

"Impossible, old fellow," replied Barbicane.

A few moments later, the three travellers had installed themselves in the projectile and screwed down the door-plates. The mouth of the *Columbiad*, cleared of all obstructions, was open to the sky.

Who could ever describe the universal excitement which had now reached its peak?

The moon was moving across a limpid sky, extinguishing the glittering stars on its way. It was now crossing the *Gemini* constellation and was nearly half way between the horizon and the zenith. It was easy for everyone to understand that the projectile was going to be aimed ahead of its target, as the hunter aims in front of the hare he wants to hit.

A terrifying silence hung over the whole scene. There was not a breath of wind on the earth; not a breath of air in any breast. Hearts no longer dared to beat. The crowd's fearful eyes were fixed on the gaping mouth of the *Columbiad*.

Murchison was watching the hand of his chronometer. There were barely forty seconds before the moment of departure, and each one of them was like a century.

At the twentieth second, a quiver ran through the crowd as it occurred to everybody that the daring travellers inside the projectile were also counting the terrible seconds. Isolated cries broke out:

"Thirty-five! . . . Thirty-six! . . . Thirty-seven! . . .Thirty-eight! . . . Thirty-nine! . . . Forty! Fire!"

Murchison pressed the switch, restoring the current and sending an electric spark into the depths of the *Columbiad*.

Instantly there was a terrifying, fantastic, superhuman explosion which could not be compared to any known sound, not even a clap of thunder or the roar of an eruption. An immense jet of flame shot from the bowels of the earth as from a crater. The ground heaved, and only a few people caught a brief glimpse of the projectile victoriously cleaving the air in the midst of clouds of blazing vapour.

With the Night Mail

RUDYARD KIPLING

This story, written about seventy years ago, is sheer science-fiction and was sub-titled A story of 2000 A.D. *Kipling, great writer that he was, had a remarkable ability to master any subject he was describing, whether it was the life of bees, or bridge-building, or engineering. He was a very early motor-car user, having what he called "a Victoria-hooded, carriage-sprung, carriage-braked, single-cylinder, belt-driven, fixed-ignition Embryo which, at times, could cover eight miles an hour."*

At nine o'clock of a gusty winter night I stood on the lower stages of one of the G.P.O. outward mail towers. My purpose was a run to Quebec in 'Postal Packet 162 or such other as may be appointed', and the Postmaster-General himself countersigned the order. This talisman opened all doors, even those in the dispatching-caisson at the foot of the tower, where they were delivering the sorted Continental mail. The bags lay packed close as herrings in the long grey underbodies which our G.P.O. still calls 'coaches.' Five such coaches were filled as I watched, and were shot up the guides to be locked on to their waiting packets, three hundred feet nearer the stars.

From the dispatching-caisson I was conducted by a courteous and wonderfully-learned official—Mr L. L. Geary, Second Dispatcher of the Western Route—to the Captains' Room (this wakes an echo of old romance), where the mail captains come on for their turn of duty. He introduces me to the Captain of '162'—Captain Purnall, and his relief, Captain Hodgson. The one is small and dark; the other large and red; but each has the brooding, sheathed glance characteristic of eagles and aeronauts. You can see it in the pictures of our racing professionals, from L. V. Tautsch to little Ada Warrleigh—that fathomless abstraction of eyes habitually turned through naked space.

On the notice-board in the Captains' Room, the pulsing arrows of some twenty indicators register, degree by geographical degree, the progress of as many homeward-bound packets. The word 'Cape' rises across the face of a dial; a gong strikes: the South African mid-weekly mail is in at the Highgate Receiving Towers. That is all. It reminds one comically of the traitorous little bell which in pigeon-fanciers' lofts notifies the return of a homer.

"Time for us to be on the move," says Captain Purnall, and we are shot up by the passenger-lift to the top of the dispatch-towers. "Our coach will lock on when it is filled and the clerks are aboard."

No. 162 waits for us in Slip E of the topmost stage. The great curve of her back shines frostily under the lights, and some minute alteration of trim makes her rock a little in her holding-down clips.

Captain Purnall frowns and dives inside. Hissing softly, '162' comes to rest as level as a rule. From her North Atlantic winter nose-cap (worn bright as diamond with boring through uncounted leagues of hail, snow, and ice) to the inset of her three built-out propeller-shafts is some 240 feet. Her extreme diameter, carried well forward, is thirty-seven. Contrast this with the nine hundred by ninety-five of any crack liner, and you will realize the power that must drive a hull through all weathers at more than the emergency speed of the *Cyclonic*!

The eye detects no joint in her skin plating save the sweeping hair-crack of the bow-rudder—Magniac's rudder that assured us the dominion of the unstable air and left its inventor penniless and half-blind. It is calculated to Castelli's 'gull-wing' curve. Raise a few feet of that all but invisible plate three-eighths of an inch and she will yaw five miles to port or starboard ere she is under control again. Give her full helm and she returns on her track like a whip-lash. Cant the whole forward—a touch on the wheel will suffice—and she sweeps at your good direction up or down. Open the complete circle and she presents to the air a mushroom-head that will bring her up all standing within a half-mile.

"Yes," says Captain Hodgson, answering my thought, "Castelli thought he'd discovered the secret of controlling aeroplanes when he'd only found out how to steer dirigible balloons. Magniac invented his rudder to help war-boats ram each other; and war went out of fashion and Magniac, he went out of his mind, because he said he couldn't serve his country any more. I wonder if any of us ever know what we're really doing."

"If you want to see the coach locked, you'd better go aboard. It's due now," says Mr Geary. I enter through the door amidships. There is nothing here for display. The inner skin of the gas-tanks comes down to within a foot or two of my head and turns over just short of the turn of the bilges. Liners and yachts disguise their tanks with decoration, but the G.P.O. serves them raw, under a lick of grey, official paint. The inner skin shuts off fifty feet of the bow and as much of the stern, but the bow-bulkhead is recessed for the lift-shunting apparatus as the stern is pierced for the shaft-tunnels. The engine-room lies almost amidships. Forward of it, extending to the turn of the bow tanks, is an aperture—a bottomless hatch at present—into which our coach will be locked. One looks down over the coamings 300 feet to the dispatching-caisson whence voices boom upwards. The light below is obscured to a sound of thunder, as our coach rises on its guides. It enlarges rapidly from a postage stamp to a playing-card; to a punt and last a pontoon. The two clerks, its crew, do not even look up as it comes into place. The Quebec letters fly under their fingers and leap into the docketed racks, while both captains and Mr Geary satisfy themselves that the coach is locked home. A clerk passes the way-bill over the hatch-coaming. Captain Purnall thumb-marks and passes it to Mr Geary. Receipt has been given and taken. "Pleasant run," says Mr Geary, and disappears through the door which a foot-high pneumatic compressor locks after him.

"A-ah!" sighs the compressor, released. Our holding-down clips part with a tang. We are clear.

Captain Hodgson opens the great colloid underbody-porthole through which I watch overlighted London slide eastward as the gale gets hold of us. The first of the low winter clouds cuts off the well-known view and darkens Middlesex. On the south edge of it I can see a postal packet's light ploughing through the white fleece. For an instant she gleams like a star ere she drops toward the Highgate Receiving Towers. "The Bombay Mail," says Captain Hodgson, and looks at his watch. "She's forty minutes late."

"What's our level?" I ask.

"Four thousand. Aren't you coming up on the bridge?"

The bridge (let us ever praise the G.P.O. as a repository of ancientest tradition!) is represented by a view of Captain Hodgson's legs where he stands on the Control Platform that runs thwartships overhead. The bow colloid is unshuttered and Captain Purnall, one hand on the wheel, is feeling for a fair slant. The dial shows 4300 feet.

"It's steep tonight," he mutters, as tier on tier of cloud

drops under. "We generally pick up an easterly draught below three thousand at this time o' the year. I hate slathering through fluff."

"So does Van Cutsen. Look at him huntin' for a slant!" says Captain Hodgson. A fog-light breaks cloud 100 fathoms below. The Antwerp Night Mail makes her signal and rises between two racing clouds far to port, her flanks blood-red in the glare of Sheerness Double Light. The gale will have us over the North Sea in half an hour, but Captain Purnall lets her go composedly—nosing to every point of the compass as she rises.

Five thousand—six, six thousand eight hundred—the dip-dial reads ere we find the easterly drift, heralded by a flurry of snow at the thousand fathom level. Captain Purnall rings up the engines and keys down the governor on the switch before him. There is no sense in urging machinery when Aeolus himself gives you good knots for nothing. We are away in earnest now—our nose notched home on our chosen star. At this level the lower clouds are laid out, all neatly combed by the dry fingers of the east. Below that again is the strong westerly blow through which we rose. Overhead, a film of southerly drifting mist draws a theatrical gauze across the firmament. The moonlight turns the lower strata to silver without a stain, except where our shadow under-runs us. Bristol and Cardiff Double Lights (those statelily inclined beams over Severnmouth) are dead ahead of us; for we keep the Southern Winter Route. Coventry Central, the pivot of the English system, stabs upward once in ten seconds its spear of diamond light to the north; and a point or two off our starboard bow the Leek, the great cloud-breaker of Saint David's Head, swings its unmistakable green beam twenty-five degrees each way. There must be half a mile of fluff over it in this weather, but it does not affect the Leek.

"Our planet's overlighted, if anything," says Captain Purnall at the wheel, as Cardiff–Bristol slides under. "I remember the old days of common white verticals that 'ud show two or three hundred feet up in a mist, if you knew where to look for 'em. In really fluffy weather they might as well have been under your hat. One could get lost coming home then, an' have some fun. Now, it's like driving down Piccadilly."

He points to the pillars of light where the cloud-breakers bore through the cloud-floor. We see nothing of England's outlines; only a white pavement pierced in all directions by these manholes of variously-coloured fire—Holy Island's white and red—St Bee's interrupted white, and so on as far as the eye can reach. Blessed be Sargent, Ahrens, and the Dubois brothers, who invented the cloud-breakers of the world whereby we travel in security!

"Are you going to lift for The Shamrock?" asks Captain Hodgson. Cork Light (green, fixed) enlarges as we rush to it. Captain Purnall nods. There is heavy traffic hereabouts— the cloud-bank beneath us is streaked with running fissures of flame where the Atlantic boats are hurrying London-ward, just clear of the fluff. Mail-packets are supposed, under the Conference rules, to have the 5000-foot lanes to themselves, but the foreigner in a hurry is apt to take liberties with English air. No. 162 lifts to a long-drawn wail of the breeze in the fore-flange of the rudder and we make Valencia (white, green, white) at a safe 7000 feet, dipping our beam to an incoming Washington packet.

There is no cloud on the Atlantic, and faint streaks of cream round Dingle Bay show where the driven seas hammer the coast. A big S.A.T.A. liner (*Societé Anonyme des Transports Aériens*) is diving and lifting half a mile below us, in search of some break in the solid west wind. Lower still lies a disabled Dane: she is telling the liner all about it in

International. Our General Communication dial has caught her talk and begins to eavesdrop. Captain Hodgson makes a motion to shut it off but checks himself. "Perhaps you'd like to listen," he says.

"*Argol* of St. Thomas," the Dane whimpers. "Report owners three starboard shaft collar-bearings fused. Can make Flores as we are, but impossible further. Shall we buy spares at Fayal?"

The liner acknowledges and recommends inverting the bearings. The *Argol* answers that she has already done so without effect and begins to relieve her mind about cheap German enamels for collar-bearings. The Frenchman assents cordially, cries "*Courage, mon ami*," and switches off.

Their lights sink under the curve of the ocean.

"That's one of Lundt & Bleamers's boats," says Captain Hodgson. "Serves 'em right for putting German compo's in their thrust-blocks. *She* won't be in Fayal to-night! By the way, wouldn't you like to look round the engine-room?"

I have been waiting eagerly for this invitation and I follow Captain Hodgson from the control-platform, stooping low to avoid the bulge of the tanks. We know that Fleury's gas can lift anything, as the world-famous trials of '89 showed, but its almost indefinite powers of expansion necessitate vast tank room. Even in this thin air the lift-shunts are busy taking out one-third of its normal lift, and still '162' must be checked by an occasional down-draw of the rudder, or our flight would become a climb to the stars. Captain Purnall prefers an overlifted to an underlifted ship; but no two captains trim ship alike. "When *I* take the bridge," says Captain Hodgson, "you'll see me shunt forty per cent of the lift out of the gas and run her on the upper rudder. With a swoop upwards instead of a swoop downwards, *as* you say. Either way will do. It's only habit. Watch our dip-dial! Tim fetches her down once every thirty knots, as regularly as breathing."

So it is shown on the dip-dial. For five or six minutes the arrow creeps from 6700 to 7300. There is the faint 'szgee' of the rudder, and back slides the arrow to 6000 on a falling slant of ten or fifteen knots.

"In heavy weather you jockey her with the screws as well," says Captain Hodgson, and, unclipping the jointed bar which divides the engine-room from the bare deck, he leads me on to the floor.

Here we find Fleury's *Paradox of the Bulk-headed Vacuum*—which we accept now without thought—literally in full blast. The three engines are H. T. & T. assisted-vaco Fleury turbines running from 3000 to the limit—that is to say, up to the point when the blades make the air 'bell'—cut out a vacuum for themselves precisely as over-driven marine propellers used to do. '162's limit is low, on account of the small size of her nine screws, which, though handier than the old colloid Thelussons, 'bell' sooner. The midships engine, generally used as a reinforce, is not running; so the port and starboard turbine vacuum-chambers draw direct into the return-mains.

The turbines whistle reflectively. From the low-arched expansion-tanks on either side, the valves descend pillar-wise to the turbine-chests, and thence the obedient gas whirls through the spirals of blades with a force that would whip the teeth out of a power-saw. Behind, is its own pressure held in leash or spurred on by the lift-shunts; before it, the vacuum where Fleury's Ray dances in violet-green bands and whirled tourbillions of flame. The jointed U-tubes of the vacuum-chamber are pressure-tempered colloid (no glass would endure the strain for an instant) and a junior engineer with tinted spectacles watches the Ray intently. It is the very heart of the machine—a mystery to this day. Even Fleury who begat it and, unlike Magniac, died a multi-millionaire, could not explain how the restless little imp shuddering in the

H

U-tube can, in the fractional fraction of a second, strike the furious blast of gas into a chill greyish-green liquid that drains (you can hear it trickle) from the far end of the vacuum to the bilges. Here it returns to its gaseous, one had almost written sagacious, state and climbs to work afresh. Bilge-tank, upper-tank, dorsal-tank, expansion-chamber, vacuum, main-return (as a liquid), and bilge-tank once more is the ordained cycle. Fleury's Ray sees to that; and the engineer with the tinted spectacles sees to Fleury's Ray. If a speck of oil, if even the natural grease of the human finger touches the hooded terminals, Fleury's Ray will wink and disappear and must be laboriously built up again. This means half a day's work for all hands and an expense of about £170 to the G.P.O. for radium-salts and such trifles.

"Now look at our thrust-collars. You won't find much German compo there. Full-jewelled, you see," says Captain Hodgson as the engineer shunts open the top of a cap. Our shaft-bearings are C.M.C. (Commercial Minerals Company) stones, ground with as much care as the lens of a telescope. They cost £37 apiece. So far we have not arrived at their term of life. These bearings came from No. 97, which took them over from the old *Dominion of Light* which had them out of the wreck of the Perseus aeroplane in the years when men still flew wooden kites over oil engines!

They are a shining reproof to all low-grade German 'ruby' enamels, so-called *boort* facings, and the dangerous and unsatisfactory alumina compounds which please dividend-hunting owners and turn skippers crazy.

The rudder-gear and the gas lift-shunt, seated side by side under the engine-room dials, are the only machines in visible motion. The former sighs from time to time, as the oil plunger rises and falls half an inch. The latter, cased and guarded like the U-tube aft, exhibits another Fleury Ray, but inverted and more green than violet. Its function is to shunt the lift out of the gas, and this it will do without watching. That is all! A tiny pump-rod wheezing and shining to itself beside a sputtering green lamp. A hundred and fifty feet aft down the flat-topped tunnel of the tanks a violet light, restless and irresolute. Between the two, three white-painted turbine-trunks, like eel-baskets laid on their sides, accentuate the empty perspectives. You can hear the trickle of the liquefied gas flowing from the vacuum into the bilge-tanks and the soft 'gluck-glock' of gas-locks closing as Captain Purnall brings '162' down by the head. The hum of the turbines and the boom of the air on our skin is no more than a cotton wool wrapping to the universal stillness. And we are running an eighteen-second mile.

I peer from the fore end of the engine-room over the hatch-coamings into the coach. The mail-clerks are sorting the Winnipeg, Calgary, and Medicine Hat bags; but there is a pack of cards ready on the table.

Suddenly a bell trills; the engineers run to the turbine-valves and stand by; but the spectacled slave of the Ray in the U-tube never lifts his head. He must watch where he is. We are hard-braked and going astern; there is language from the Control Platform.

"Tim's sparking badly about something," says the unruffled Captain Hodgson. "Let's look."

Captain Purnall is not the suave man we left half an hour since, but the embodied authority of the G.P.O. Ahead of us floats an ancient aluminium-patched, twin-screw tramp of the dingiest, with no more right to the 5000-foot lane than has a horse-cart to a modern road. She carries an obsolete *barbette* conning-tower—a six-foot affair with railed platform forward—and our warning beam plays on the top of it as a policeman's lantern flashes on the area sneak. Like a sneak-thief, too, emerges a shock-headed navigator in his shirt-sleeves. Captain Purnall wrenches open the colloid to talk to him, man to man. There are times when Science does not satisfy.

"What under the stars are you doing here, you sky-scraping chimney-sweep?" he shouts as we two drift, side by side. "Do you know this is a mail-lane? You call yourself a sailor, sir? You ain't fit to peddle toy balloons to an Eskimo. Your name and number! Report and get down, and be—!"

"I've been blown up once," the shock-headed man cries, hoarsely, as a dog barking. "I don't care two flips of a contact for anything *you* can do, Postie."

"Don't you sir? But I'll make you care. I'll have you towed stern first to Disko and broke up. You can't recover insurance if you're broke for obstruction. Do you understand *that*?"

Then the stranger bellows, "Look at my propellers! There's been a wulli-wa down below that has knocked us into umbrella-frames! We've been blown up about forty thousand feet! We're all one conjuror's watch inside! My mate's arm's broke; my engineer's head cut open; my Ray went out when the engines smashed; and ... and ... for pity's sake give me my height! We doubt we're dropping."

"We ought to blow into St John's with luck. We're trying

"Six thousand eight hundred. Can you hold it?" Captain Purnall overlooks all insults, and leans half out of the colloid, staring and snuffing. The stranger leaks pungently.

We ought to blow into St John's with luck. We're trying to plug the foretank now, but she's simply whistling it away," her captain wails.

"She's sinking like a log," says Captain Purnall in an undertone. "Call up the Banks Mark Boat, George." Our dip-dial shows that we, keeping abreast the tramp, have dropped 500 feet the last few minutes.

Captain Purnall presses a switch and our signal beam begins to swing through the night, twizzling spokes of light across infinity.

"That'll fetch something," he says, while Captain Hodgson watches the General Communicator. He has called up the North Banks Mark Boat, a few hundred miles west, and is reporting the case.

"I'll stand by you," Captain Purnall roars to the lone figure on the conning-tower.

"Is it as bad as that?" comes the answer. "She isn't insured. She's mine."

"Might have guessed as much," mutters Hodgson. "Owner's risk is the worst risk of all!"

"Can't I fetch St. John's—not even with this breeze?" the voice quavers.

"Stand by to abandon ship. Haven't you *any* lift in you, fore or aft?"

"Nothing but the midship tanks, and they're none too tight. You see, my Ray gave out and—" he coughs in the reek of the escaping gas.

"You poor devil!" This does not reach our friend. "What does the Mark Boat say, George?"

"Wants to know if there's any danger to traffic. Says she's in a bit of weather herself and can't quit station. I've turned in a General Call, so even if they don't see our beam, someone's bound to help—or else *we* must. Shall I clear our slings? Hold on! Here we are! A Planet liner, too! She'll be up in a tick!"

"Tell her to have her slings ready," cries his brother captain. "There won't be much time to spare . . . Tie up your mate," he roars to the tramp.

"My mate's all right. It's my engineer. He's gone crazy."

"Shunt the lift out of him with a spanner. Hurry!"

"But I can make St John's if you'll stand by."

"You'll make the deep, wet Atlantic in twenty minutes. You're less than 5800 now. Get your papers."

A Planet liner, eastbound, heaves up in a superb spiral and

takes the air of us humming. Her underbody colloid is open and her transporter-slings hang down like tentacles. We shut off our beam as she adjusts herself—steering to a hair—over the tramp's conning-tower. The mate comes up, his arm strapped to his side, and stumbles into the cradle. A man with a ghastly scarlet head follows, shouting that he must go back and build up his Ray. The mate assures him that he will find a nice new Ray all ready in the liner's engine-room. The bandaged head goes up wagging excitedly. A youth and a woman follow. The liner cheers hollowly above us, and we see the passengers' faces at the saloon colloid.

"That's a pretty girl. What's the fool waiting for now?" says Captain Purnall.

The Skipper comes up, still appealing to us to stand by and see him fetch St. John's. He dives below and returns—at which we little human beings in the void cheer louder than ever—with the ship's kitten. Up fly the liner's hissing slings; her underbody crashes home and she hurtles away again. The dial shows less than 3000 feet.

The Mark Boat signals we must attend to the derelict, now whistling her death-song, as she falls beneath us in long, sick zigzags.

"Keep our beam on her and send out a General Warning," says Captain Purnall, following her down.

There is no need. Not a liner in air but knows the meaning of that vertical beam and gives us and our quarry a wide berth.

"But she'll drown in the water, won't she?" I ask.

"Not always," is his answer. "I've known a derelict up-end and sift her engines out of herself and flicker round the lower lanes for three weeks on her forward tanks only. We'll run no risks. Pith her, George, and look sharp. There's weather ahead."

Captain Hodgson opens the underbody colloid, swings

the heavy pithing-iron out of its rack, which in liners is generally cased as a smoking-room settee, and at 200 feet releases the catch. We hear the whirr of the crescent-shaped arms opening as they descend. The derelict's forehead is punched in, starred across, and rent diagonally. She falls stern first, our beam upon her, slides like a lost soul down that pitiless ladder of light, and the Atlantic takes her.

"A filthy business," says Hodgson. "I wonder what it must have been like in the old days?"

The thought had crossed my mind, too. What if that wavering carcass had been filled with the men of the old days, each one of them taught (*that* is the horror of it!) that after death he would very possibly go for ever to unspeakable torment?

And scarcely a generation ago, we (one knows now that we are only our fathers re-enlarged upon the earth), *we*, I say, ripped and rammed and pithed to admiration.

Here Tim, from the Control Platform, shouts that we are to get into our inflators and to bring him his at once.

We hurry into the heavy rubber suits—the engineers are already dressed—and inflate at the air-pump taps. G.P.O. inflators are thrice as thick as a racing man's "flickers," and chafe abominably under the armpits. George takes the wheel until Tim has blown himself up to the extreme of rotundity. If you kicked him off the C.P. to the deck he would bounce back. But it is '162' that will do the kicking.

"The Mark Boat's mad—stark ravin' crazy," he snorts, returning to command. "She says there's a bad blow-out ahead and wants me to pull over to Greenland. I'll see her pithed first! We wasted half an hour fussing over that dead duck down under, and now I'm expected to go rubbin' my back all round the Pole. What does she think a postal packet's made of? Gummed silk? Tell her we're coming on straight, George."

119

George buckles him into the Frame and switches on the Direct Control. Now under Tim's left toe lies the port-engine Accelerator; under his left heel the Reverse, and so with the other foot. The lift-shunt stops stand out on the rim of the steering-wheel, where the fingers of his left hand can play on them. At his right hand is the midships engine-lever, ready to be thrown into gear at a moment's notice. He leans forward in his belt, eyes glued to the colloid, and one ear cocked toward the General Communicator. Henceforth he is the strength and direction of '162', through whatever may befall.

The Banks Mark Boat is reeling out pages of A.B.C. Directions to the traffic at large. We are to secure all 'loose objects'; hood up our Fleury Rays; and on no account to attempt to clear snow from our conning-towers till the weather abates. Underpowered craft, we are told, can ascend to the limit of their lift, mail-packets to look out for them accordingly; the lower lanes westward are pitting very badly, 'with frequent blow-outs, vortices, laterals, etc.'

Still the clear dark holds up unblemished. The only warning is the electric skin-tension (I feel as though I were a lace-maker's pillow) and an irritability which the gibbering of the General Communicator increases almost to hysteria.

We have made 8000 feet since we pithed the tramp and our turbines are giving us an honest 210 knots.

Very far to the west an elongated blur of red, low down, shows us the North Banks Mark Boat. There are specks of fire round her, rising and falling—bewildered planets about an unstable sun—helpless shipping hanging on to her light for company's sake. No wonder she could not quit station.

She warns us to look out for the backwash of the bad vortex in which (her beam shows it) she is even now reeling.

The pits of gloom about us begin to fill with very faintly luminous films—wreathing and uneasy shapes. One forms itself into a globe of pale flame that waits, shivering with eagerness, till we sweep by. It leaps monstrously across the blackness, alights on the precise tip of our nose, pirouettes there an instant, and swings off. Our roaring bow sinks as though that light were lead—sinks and recovers, to lurch and stumble again beneath the next blow-out. Tim's fingers on the lift-shunt strike chords of numbers—1:4:7: − 2:4:6: − 7:5:3, and so on; for he is running by his tanks only, lifting or lowering her against the uneasy air. All three engines are at work, for the sooner we have skated over this thin ice the better. Higher we dare not go. The whole upper vault is charged with pale krypton vapours, which our skin friction may excite to unholy manifestations. Between the upper and lower levels—5000 and 7000, hints the Mark Boat—we may perhaps bolt through if . . . Our bow clothes itself in blue flame and falls like a sword. No human skill can keep pace with the changing tensions. A vortex has us by the beak and we dive down a 2000-foot slant at an angle (the dip-dial and my bouncing body record it) of thirty-five. Our turbines scream shrilly; the propellers cannot bite on the thin air; Tim shunts the lift out of five tanks at once and by sheer weight, drives her bullet-wise through the maelstrom till she cushions with a jar on an up-gust, 3000 feet below.

"*Now* we've done it," says George in my ear. "Our skin-friction, that last slide, has played Old Harry with the tensions! Look out for laterals, Tim; she'll want some holding."

"I've got her," is the answer. "Come *up*, old woman."

She comes up nobly, but the laterals buffet her left and right like the pinions of angry angels. She is jolted off her course four ways at once, and cuffed into place again, only to be swung aside and dropped into a new chaos. We are never without a corposant grinning on our bows or rolling head over heels from nose to midships, and to the crackle of electricity around and within us is added once or twice the rattle of hail—hail that will never fall on any sea. Slow we must or we may break our back, pitch-poling.

"Air's a perfectly elastic fluid," roars George above the tumult. "About as elastic as a head sea off the Fastnet, ain't it?"

He is less than just to the good element. If one intrudes on the heavens when they are balancing their volt-accounts; if one disturbs the High Gods' market-rates by hurling steel hulls at ninety knots across tremblingly-adjusted electric tensions, one must not complain of any rudeness in the reception. Tim met it with an unmoved countenance, one corner of his under lip caught up on a tooth, his eyes fleeting into the blackness twenty miles ahead, and the fierce sparks flying from his knuckles at every turn of the hand. Now and again he shook his head to clear the sweat trickling from his eyebrows, and it was then that George, watching his chance, would slide down the life-rail and swab his face quickly with a big red handkerchief. I never imagined that a human being could so continuously labour and so collectedly think as did Tim through that Hell's half-hour when the flurry was at its worst. We were dragged hither and yon by warm or frozen suctions, belched up on the tops of wulli-was, spun down by vortices and clubbed aside by laterals under a dizzying rush of stars in the company of a drunken moon. I heard the rushing click of the midship-engine-lever sliding in and out, the low growl of the lift-shunts, and, louder than the yelling winds without, the scream of the bow-rudder gouging into any lull that promised hold for an instant. At last we began to claw up on a cant, bow-rudder and port-propeller together; only the nicest balancing of tanks saved us from spinning like the rifle-bullet of the old days.

"We've got to hitch to windward of that Mark Boat somehow," George cried.

"There's no windward," I protested feebly, where I swung shackled to a stanchion. "How can there be?"

He laughed—as we pitched into a 1000-foot blow-out—
that red man laughed beneath his inflated hood!

"Look!" he said. "We must clear those refugees with a
high lift."

The Mark Boat was below and a little to the sou'west of us,
fluctuating in the centre of her distraught galaxy. The air
was thick with moving lights at every level. I take it most of
them were trying to lie head to wind but, not being hydras,
they failed. An undertanked Moghrabi boat had risen to
the limit of her lift, and, finding no improvement, had
dropped a couple of thousand. There she met a superb wulli-
wa, and was blown up spinning like a dead leaf. Instead of
shutting off she went astern and, naturally, rebounded as
from a wall almost into the Mark Boat, whose language
(our G.C. took it in) was humanly simple.

"If they'd only ride it out quietly it 'ud be better," said
George in a calm, while we climbed like a bat above them
all. "But some skippers *will* navigate without enough lift.
What does that Tad-boat think she is doing, Tim?"

"Playing kiss in the ring," was Tim's unmoved reply. A
Trans-Asiatic Direct liner had found a smooth and butted
into it full power. But there was a vortex at the tail of that
smooth, so the T.A.D. was flipped out like a pea from off a
fingernail, braking madly as she fled down and all but
overending."

"Now I hope she's satisfied," said Tim. "I'm glad I'm
not a Mark Boat . . . Do I want help?" The General Communicator dial had caught his ear. "George, you may tell
that gentleman with my love—love, remember, George—
that I do not want help. Who *is* the officious sardine-tin?"

"A Rimouski drogher on the look-out for a tow."

"Very kind of the Rimouski drogher. This postal packet
isn't being towed at present."

"Those droghers will go anywhere on a chance of salvage,"

George explained. "We call 'em 'kittiwakes'."

A long-beaked, bright steel ninety-footer floated at ease for one instant within hail of us, her slings coiled ready for rescues, and a single hand in her open tower. He was smoking. Surrendered to the insurrection of the airs through which we tore our way, he lay in absolute peace. I saw the smoke of his pipe ascend untroubled ere his boat dropped, it seemed, like a stone in a well.

We had just cleared the Mark Boat and her disorderly neighbours when the storm ended as suddenly as it had begun. A shooting-star to northward filled the sky with the luminous green blink of a meteorite dissipating itself in our atmosphere.

Said George, "That may iron out all the tensions." Even as he spoke, the conflicting winds came to rest; the levels filled; the laterals died out in long easy swells; the airways were smoothed before us. In less than three minutes the covey round the Mark Boat had shipped their power-lights and whirred away upon their businesses.

"What's happened?" I gasped. The nerve-storm within and the volt-tingle without had passed: my inflators weighed like lead.

"God, He knows!" said Captain George soberly. "That old shooting-star's skin-friction has discharged the different levels. I've seen it happen before. Phew! What a relief!"

We dropped from 10000 to 6000 and got rid of our clammy suits. Tim shut off and stepped out of the Frame. The Mark Boat was coming up behind us. He opened the colloid in that heavenly stillness and mopped his face.

"Hello, Williams!" he cried. "A degree or two out o' station, ain't you?"

"Maybe," was the answer from the Mark Boat. "I've had some company this evening."

"So I noticed. Wasn't that quite a little draught?"

"I warned you. Why didn't you pull out north? The eastbound packets have."

"Me? Not till I'm running a Polar consumptives' sanatorium boat. I was squinting through a colloid before you were out of your cradle, my son."

"I'd be the last man to deny it," the captain of the Mark Boat replies softly. "The way you handled her just now—I'm a pretty fair judge of traffic in a volt-flurry—it was 1000 revolutions beyond anything even *I've* ever seen."

Tim's back supples visibly to this oiling. Captain George on the C.P. winks and points to the portrait of a singularly attractive maiden pinned up on Tim's telescope-bracket above the steering-wheel.

I see. Wholly and entirely do I see!

There is some talk overhead of "coming round to tea on Friday," a brief report of the derelict's fate, and Tim volunteers as he descends: "For an A.B.C. man, young Williams is less of a high-tension fool than some . . . . Were you thinking of taking her on, George? Then I'll just have a look round that port-thrust—seems to me it's a trifle warm—and we'll jog along."

The Mark Boat hums off joyously and hangs herself up in her appointed eyrie. Here she will stay, a shutterless observatory; a lifeboat station; a salvage tug; a court of ultimate appeal-cum-meteorological bureau for 300 miles in all directions, till Wednesday next when her relief slides across the stars to take her buffeted place. Her black hull, double conning-tower, and ever-ready slings represent all that remains to the planet of that odd old world authority. She is responsible only to the Aerial Board of Control—the A.B.C. of which Tim speaks so flippantly. But that semi-elected, semi-nominated body of a few score persons of both sexes, controls this planet. "Transportation is Civilization," our motto runs. Theoretically, we do what we please so long as

125

we do not interfere with the traffic *and all it implies*. Practically, the A.B.C. confirms or annuls all international arrangements and, to judge from its last report, finds our tolerant, humorous, lazy little planet only too ready to shift the whole burden of public administration on its shoulders.

I discuss this with Tim, sipping maté on the C.P. while George fans her along over the white blur of the Banks in beautiful, upward curves of fifty miles each. The dip-dial translates them on the tape in flowing freehand.

Tim gathers up a skein of it and surveys the last few feet, which record '162's' path through the volt-flurry.

"I haven't had a fever-chart like this to show up in five years," he says ruefully.

A postal packet's dip-dial records every yard of every run. The tapes then go to the A.B.C., which collates and makes composite photographs of them for the instruction of captains. Tim studies his irrevocable past, shaking his head.

"Hello! Here's a 1500-foot drop at fifty-five degrees! We must have been standing on our heads then, George."

"You don't say so," George answers. "I fancied I noticed it at the time."

George may not have Captain Purnall's catlike swiftness, but he is all artist, to the tips of the broad fingers that play on the shunt-stops. The delicious flight-curves come away on the tape with never a waver. The Mark Boat's vertical spindle of light lies down to eastward, setting in the face of the following stars. Westward, where no planet should rise, the triple verticals of Trinity Bay (we keep still to the southern route) make a low-lifting haze. We seem the only thing at rest under all the heavens; floating at ease till the earth's revolution shall turn up our landing-towers.

Our silent clock gives us a sixteen-second mile.

"Some fine night," says Tim, "we'll be even with that clock's Master."

"He's coming now," says George, over his shoulder. "I'm chasing the night west."

The stars ahead dim no more than if a film of mist had been drawn under, unobserved, but the deep air-boom on our skin changes to a joyful shout.

"The dawn-gust," says Tim. "It'll go on to meet the Sun. Look! Look! There's the dark being crammed back over our bows! Come to the after-colloid. I'll show you something."

The engine-room is hot and stuffy; the clerks in the coach asleep; and the Slave of the Ray is ready to follow them. Tim slides open the aft colloid and reveals the curve of the world—the ocean's deepest purple—edged with fuming and intolerable gold. Then the Sun rises and through the colloid strikes out our lamps. Tim scowls in his face.

"Squirrels in a cage," he mutters. "That's all we are. Squirrels in a cage! He's going twice as fast as us. Just you wait a few years, my shining friend, and we'll take steps that will amaze you. *We'll* Joshua you!"

Yes, that is our dream: to turn all earth into the Vale of Ajalon at our pleasure. So far, we can drag out the dawn to twice its normal length in these latitudes. But some day— even on the Equator—we shall hold the Sun level in his full stride.

Now we look down on a sea thronged with heavy traffic. A big submersible breaks water suddenly. Another and another follows with a swash and a suck and a savage bubbling of relieved pressures. The deep-sea freighters are rising to lung-up after the long night, and the leisurely ocean is all patterned with peacocks' eyes of foam.

"We'll lung-up, too," says Tim, and when we return to the C.P. George shuts off, the colloids are opened, and the fresh air sweeps her out. There is no hurry. The old contracts (they will be revised at the end of the year) allow twelve hours for a run which any packet can put behind her in ten. So we breakfast in the arms of an easterly slant which pushes us along at a languid twenty.

To enjoy life, and tobacco, begin both on a sunny morning half a mile or so above the dappled Atlantic cloud-belts and after a volt-flurry which has cleared and tempered your nerves. While we discussed the thickening traffic with the superiority that comes of having a high level reserved to ourselves, we heard (and I for the first time) the morning hymn on a Hospital boat.

She was cloaked by a skein of ravelled fluff beneath us and we caught the chant before she rose into the sunlight. *"O ye Winds of God,"* sang the unseen voices, *"bless ye the Lord! Praise Him and magnify Him for ever!"*

We slid off our caps and joined in. When our shadow fell across her great open platforms they looked up and stretched out their hands neighbourly while they sang. We could see the doctors and the nurses and the white, button-like faces of the cot-patients. She passed slowly beneath us, heading northward, her hull, wet with the dews of the night, all ablaze in the sunshine. So took she the shadow of a cloud and vanished, her song continuing. *"O ye holy and humble men of heart, bless ye the Lord! Praise Him and magnify Him for ever."*

"She's a public lunger or she wouldn't have been singing the *Benedicite*; and she's a Greenlander or she wouldn't have snow-blinds over her colloids," said George at last. "She'll be bound for Frederikshavn or one of the Glacier sanatoriums for a month. If she was an accident ward she'd be hung up at the 8000-foot level. Yes—consumptives."

"Funny how the new things are the old things. I've read in books," Tim answered, "that savages used to haul their sick and wounded up to the tops of hills because microbes were fewer there. We hoist 'em into sterilized air for a while. Same idea. How much do the doctors say we've added to the average life of a man?"

"Thirty years," says George with a twinkle in his eye. "Are we going to spend 'em all up here, Tim?"

"Flap ahead, then. Flap ahead. Who's hindering?" the senior captain laughed, as we went in.

We held a good lift to clear the coastwise and Continental shipping; and we had need of it. Though our route is in no sense a populated one, there is a steady trickle of traffic this way along. We met Hudson Bay furriers out of the Great Preserve, hurrying to make their departure from Bonavista with sable and black fox for the insatiable markets. We over-crossed Keewatin liners, small and cramped; but their captains, who see no land between Trepassy and Blanco, know what gold they bring back from West Africa. Trans-Asiatic Directs, we met, soberly ringing the world round the Fiftieth Meridian at an honest seventy knots; and white-painted Ackroyd & Hunt fruiters out of the south fled beneath us, their ventilated hulls whistling like Chinese kites. Their market is in the north, among the northern sanatoria, where you can smell their grapefruit and bananas across the cold snows. Argentine beef boats we sighted too, of enormous capacity and unlovely outline. They, too, feed the northern health stations in ice-bound ports where submersibles dare not rise.

Yellow-bellied ore-flats and Ungava petrol-tanks punted down leisurely out of the north, like strings of unfrightened wild duck. It does not pay to 'fly' minerals and oil a mile further than is necessary; but the risks of trans-shipping to submersibles in the ice-pack off Nain or Hebron are so great that these heavy freighters fly down to Halifax direct, and scent the air as they go. They are the biggest tramps aloft, except the Athabasca grain-tubs. But these last, now that the wheat is moved, are busy, over the world's shoulder, timber-lifting in Siberia.

We held to the St. Lawrence, (it is astonishing how the

old waterways still pull us children of the air), and followed the broad line of black between its drifting ice-blocks, all down the Park that the wisdom of our fathers—but every one knows the Quebec run . . .

We dropped to the Heights Receiving Towers twenty minutes ahead of time, and there hung at east till the Yokohama Intermediate Packet could pull out and give us our proper slip. It was curious to watch the action of the holding-down clips all along the frosty river front as the boats cleared or came to rest. A big Hamburger was leaving Pont Levis and her crew, unshipping the platform railings, began to sing 'Elsinore'—the oldest of our shanties. You know it of course—

Mother Rugen's tea-house on the Baltic—
  Forty couples waltzing on the floor!
And you can watch my Ray,
For I must go away
  And dance with Ella Sweyn at Elsinore!

Then, while they sweated home the covering-plates,

Nor-Nor-Nor-Nor-
West from Sourabaya to the Baltic—
  Ninety knot an hour to the Skaw!
Mother Rugen's tea-house on the Baltic
  And a dance with Ella Sweyn at Elsinore!

The clips parted with a gesture of indignant dismissal, as though Quebec, glittering under her snows, were casting out these light and unworthy lovers. Our signal came from the Heights. Tim turned and floated up, but surely then it was with passionate appeal that the great tower arms flung open—or did I think so because on the upper staging a little hooded figure also opened her arms wide towards her father?

In ten seconds the coach with its clerks clashed down to the receiving-caisson; the hostlers displaced the engineers at the idle turbines, and Tim, prouder of this than all, introduced me to the maiden of the photograph on the shelf. "And by the way," said he to her, stepping forth in sunshine under the hat of civil life, "I saw young Williams in the Mark Boat. I've asked him to tea on Friday."

Beginner's Luck

SHEILA SCOTT

Amelia Earhart—first woman to fly the Atlantic, 1928; Amy Johnson—England to South Africa in four days, 1932; Jean Batten—England to Australia in fourteen days, 1934; Valentina Tereshkova—first woman to orbit in space, 1963 . . . The history of the human mastery of flight is studded with the names of intrepid women. Here, a present-day flier renowned for her many exploits, describes an early day in her career when she was still learning to spread her wings.

It had been a glorious weekend for the Royal Aero Club's annual rally in Deauville, France, in 1960, but now I was in a hurry to return to England, and the weather was changing. I had to get *Myth* prepared for my first attempt in the heats for the King's Cup Air Race later that week. At that time she had no radio, or artificial horizon (an instrument which tells you the altitude of the aircraft, even if you are flying in cloud), nor any type of direction gyro-indicator. I had logged a mere two hours of basic instrument flying "under the hood" in her sister, the *Tiger Moth*. One can learn very basic instrument flying and simulate flying in clouds or at night in a *Tiger Moth* by pulling a canvas hood up and over the rear cockpit whilst the instructor sits in the front cockpit out in the open to watch out for other aircraft. This training is very rudimentary and does not approach the intensive course needed for an instrument rating, but it does teach one to stay the right way up when in cloud.

I decided to fly along the coast to Cap Gris Nez and take the shortest sea crossing to Lympne. It was bumpy over the Channel and as I landed, bad weather was building up. The English airfield controller gloomily shook his head and suggested I land again half-way along my route and re-check the "Met." at Shoreham. A quick telephone call to my base at Thruxton had elicited the information that although the cloud ceiling was low, they did have several miles' visibility there, and that the hangar boys were waiting to start work on *Myth*.

Untroubled, I set off and avoided the worst weather and by squeezing through the showers on either side of me I had comparatively good visibility. Eventually, I saw the power-station chimneys of Shoreham looming up in a patch of sunshine that had escaped through the clouds. It all looked harmless enough, except for a sullen bank of dark *nimbo-stratus* (a bad weather cloud) to the west.

I still had plenty of fuel and Thruxton was only an hour's flight away. In a burst of over-confidence I decided to ignore the warning, and cut out the landing for a re-check from "Met." at Shoreham. As I flew on over the Downs, the over-cast began to look much more solid and menacing. It got very dark, and I was pushed down lower by the expanding clouds, but I flew on, regardless, as I could see clear patches lower down.

I diverted occasionally to avoid the now heavy rain, but after I had flown over an uncharted reservoir which I had never noticed before, I decided to try and return to my original course, in case I got lost. This was another mistake, but my thoughts were now only on the forthcoming race, and how much practising and preparing there was still to be done.

Soon the clouds came swirling and dipping right down to the ground and I kept getting caught up in wisps of it, however low I flew. I was still able to see some ground below, but unfortunately not enough to recognize my bearings. A twisting ribbon of railway-line snaked underneath me, but disappeared into a tunnel without divulging its secret of where we were, although it did remind me that there was higher ground ahead. I remembered from my earlier map-reading that the highest point was only about 2,000 feet above sea-level.

Rain started to lash forth in an absolute fury. I could hardly see a thing, and I was badly frightened as *Myth* bounced around the sky. I recalled the many hair-raising bar stories of other, more experienced pilots, and their oft-quoted rule "always gain height for safety". I knew I must be approaching the highest ridge and climbed a little.

This turned out to be worse; I was now in solid cloud, unable to descend to get out of it, lest I hit the hillside or one of the many electric pylons or overhead electricity cables. It surely must get better. Thruxton had said they could see for miles, so it could not be solid the whole way from Shoreham to base. If I could just survive long enough to get through this murky stuff over the ridge, I should soon be out of it. I tried desperately to remember all I had been taught about blind flying. It was little enough, and I could only remember to watch my air-speed and height which, in my now very anxious state, became most erratic. There seemed too many instruments to look at, but somehow I managed to stay above 2,000 feet.

I had completely forgotten that the pressure can change considerably in a front, and that my altimeter probably was not reading correctly. I hardly dared to look out at the now glaringly white cloud. It made my head whirl and I quickly looked back at the familiar cockpit and the numerous animals on the seat beside me given to me by well-wishers in France a few hours earlier. This steadied me a little, and I decided to keep my eyes glued to the instruments inside and not look out for a while.

I turned the navigation lights on, and the little cockpit light too, and this was comforting. I tried not to clasp the stick, because I knew the aeroplane could fly better herself than I could, providing that she was correctly trimmed. Then, to my horror, I saw the compass needle was spinning round madly. I was flying round in circles, because, in my tenseness, I had unevenly clamped my feet down on the rudders and held the stick crookedly. Luckily both were in the same direction, or it would have been the ideal set-up for a spin.

Remembering the cure for stage fright of years ago, I breathed deeply and tried to relax all my muscles. The compass needle stopped its eerie spinning, but the aeroplane was now facing the wrong way, and we were heading back to the hills. How long had we been circling? I was near to tears as I tried to make my brain recall the things I had been taught. I felt utterly alone as never before, and I talked aloud to *Myth* in a desperate attempt to find company and aid. Oddly, this helped. I gingerly turned on to the new course for what seemed an eternity, hardly daring to move the controls lest the nose went up or down too far, and we should spin off the turn.

The compass now showed a more reasonable heading, but the engine began to splutter and cough and then it seemed to roar. I had not touched the throttle, but was suddenly aware of enormous air-speed. No wonder the engine sounded louder—I was in a dive—the clouds had now swirled apart and I caught a glimpse of a tree. Feverishly fighting the controls again, I cried out aloud in sheer terror to *Myth*. I felt that I was going to be killed, but I was too frightened to climb back up into the blanket of mist. To fly in that murk would feel like suffocation, but there were pylons and trees below it which were hazardous to fly through. Why had I not taken the airfield controller's advice?

I found my shaking had stopped, now that I had faced the facts: I was angry at the thought of dying at this stage. I had got into this trouble because I had not taken enough care over my pre-flight checks, nor listened to the airfield controller's advice.

We lurched in and out of the mist again, but now it did not look so cold and unfeeling and I thought perhaps we were almost through it. Through the overcast I caught a fleeting view of a hangar with an army truck standing outside it. It was a service airfield not many miles from home. Remembering the complications and ragging of those who had landed in error there in the past, and regaining my confidence from the relief of seeing terra firma below me, I resolved to go on.

I was now able to fly very low under the cloud over the flattish ground, although I still could not see very far ahead. I could not even see the far hedges of the fields, although at least I could see enough to stay the right side up. I was hopelessly lost, and thought of a precautionary landing. This reminded me to throttle back and fly as slowly as possible, as undoubtedly this contributed to conserving my petrol. But I could not find an unobstructed field large enough to give me sufficient confidence to land. I was now extremely tired and my course became drunken and erratic again. The navigation chart had long since disappeared below the seats, out of my reach.

At last an unknown town appeared below me. The church was not the shape or colour for it to be the town of Andover which I was looking for. I looked down at the tombstones, trying not to think of the one that might be awaiting me.

Suddenly a group of modern, odd-shaped, brightly-coloured houses appeared—surely I had seen that avenue before? Indeed I had stayed there with some flying chums, only a few weekends before. It was Salisbury: I had not recognized the cathedral steeple, because it had been partially obscured by the gloom. I was miles off track, but at least there was a main railway-line from there, heading straight back to Andover Junction and passing within a mile of Thruxton airfield.

My troubles were still not over. Although I followed the railway, I did not recognize a single house or field to lead me home until I found myself over Andover. This should not have been too difficult, as there was an airfield there, too, and in any case I thought I knew all the surrounding farms by heart and estimated Thruxton to be only about ten fields away. I remembered the course setting from Andover to base and found two familiar farms. I knew I was nearly home.

Then I thought of the time and I realized I could have little or very little fuel left. I leant back to look up at the gauge on the top of the wing—it was reading zero. How long had it been registering "nothing"? In looking up at the gauge, I became utterly disorientated and lost again. I prayed that *Myth* would keep going long enough for me to find a flat field. I looked wildly around for the airfield to loom up out of the gloom, when, to my astonishment, another *Jackaroo* appeared out of the murk and flew alongside me. My instructor's face grinned cheerily at me and he indicated I was to follow him in.

My airfield had become extremely worried when the weather changed and they realized I was overdue. They telephoned all the local airports, in the hope that I had landed at one of them, but all they could find out was that one of them had heard me circling around. My instructor had taken off several times to try and find me, but the sky was too obscured and misty to see. As he stood outside on the field, wondering what to do, he heard the sound of a Gipsy engine go by, and guessed that I was following the railway and would find Andover, so he took off in that direction and carried out a square search just above the trees, until he caught up with me. Within a few minutes we were landing and I taxied unsteadily to the hangar. I got out, a shaking wreck, and was not helped by the Old Man himself appearing and giving me a tremendous rocket in front of everyone.

When the boys looked at the engine, they found that the wire in the magneto was in two pieces and by some miracle the two pieces had grated against each other and kept it going. The coughing engine had not been a pilot's imagination. We opened my flight-bag, where I had unthinkingly put a box of French matches (which were of the non-safety kind) and found that they had exploded, setting fire to one of the charts. I had not smelled it, but luckily the bag had been zipped up and the lack of oxygen had stopped the fire.

The life span of an untrained pilot on instruments in cloud is supposed to be two minutes, yet something had kept me right way up and flying for more than an hour in solid cloud. I had been airborne for 3.05 hours and the normal absolute endurance for the *Jackaroo* was 2.45 hours.

Throttling back had probably saved me from a forced landing through lack of fuel, but there was nothing to explain how I could have made so many mistakes, with the additional hazard of an ailing engine, and escaped an almost certain prang. There certainly must be something that looks after newborn pilots. Sentimentally, I believe my *Myth* sign also had a little to do with it. That was my own special sign which I had had painted on the plane and have had inscribed on every aeroplane since then. I swear by it, and believe it has saved my life on many occasions . . .

Storm over the Tasman Sea

FRANCIS CHICHESTER

Sir Francis Chichester was best known for his sailing exploits. But long before he took to ocean-yachting, he was an air-pilot with a considerable reputation. One of his earliest solo feats was carried out in 1931 when, in a frail and ramshackle Moth aeroplane which he had converted into a seaplane, he made the first-ever flight over the perilous Tasman Sea between New Zealand and Australia. Here, with typical sang-froid, he is struggling against an equally typical storm of that region.

Soon, there was an almost unbroken ceiling of cloud hanging above. It sagged like a sheet tacked up at regular intervals. The wind was increasing in force and backing persistently. At two and a half hours out the sky was completely shut off by the dull grey, threatening cloud. Dropping too, by thunder! I must definitely give up the idea of obtaining a sextant shot when three hours out. In fact the grey of the ceiling was rapidly becoming darker and lowering. I spurred myself into making some hurried drift observations. The wind was fifty m.p.h. from the north-east, by Jove! The plane would be forty-three miles off course to the south and, with the drift, was heading obliquely for the receding part of Australia. Forty-three miles! Unfortunate that I had allowed it to become so much. I at once changed course another 10 degrees to the north. Looking up, I found the clouds ahead dark, heavy grey, infused with black. And the wind was backing rapidly—a storm, by heavens! How intolerably foul! Staring ahead, I could see an apparently solid curtain right across the path of flight. I scanned it to the north, but could see no sign of a break anywhere; I searched to the south—there was not a single gap from horizon to horizon. And it hung heavily from cloud ceiling to water surface, barring my passage. I fastened the safety-belt.

I felt chilled, and made tight the scarf around my neck. At three hours less two minutes, the aeroplane struck heavy rain; it stung my face. The rate the drift was carrying the plane south was almost alarming. The wind had backed till now it was right in the north. Again I changed course another 10 degrees, which put the wind dead abeam. More than that I dare not correct—so I felt—I could not reason. My reason was quite numb or dead. But I sensed that once I began making a headwind of that gale, I destroyed my chance of reaching the mainland. Drift—40 degrees to the south, I judged. The plane was being driven half sideways, like a crab. At three hours to the instant, the plane flew into a downpour twice as heavy as the first. I had forgotten that it could rain so heavily. I kept my head down as much as possible, but the water caught the top of my helmet, streamed down my face and poured down my neck. My spirits were in the deepest depression. How I craved to escape just this sort of thing!

On the instant the plane left this downpour, which I had thought as heavy as I could possibly bear, it seemed to strike a solid wall of water with a crash. God! I ducked my head. I could see, in the corner of my eye, water leaving the wing's trailing edge in a sheet, to be shattered almost on the instant by the air blast. On either side of my head, water poured into the cockpit in two streams, which were scattered like wind-blown waterfalls and blew into my face. Immediately, I was flying as "blind" as if in a dense cloud of smoke. I throttled back till the motor was making no effort and began a slanting dive for the water. God! What a fool to let myself be caught in this, so high above the water, and yet so low. Panic clutched me! The water would be invisible in this deluge except for a few square yards vertically below, and as for that, once the plane began a turn and locked the compass needle with centrifugal force, "vertical" was no more to be recognized than "horizontal". But I must not panic—it meant dying like a paralysed rabbit. I began repeating to myself, "Keep cool! Keep cool! K-e-e-p c-o-o-l!" forming the words with my lips. The plane passed through small sudden bumps, which shook it as a terrier shakes a rat. I looked over at the strut-speed indicator for the speed of the dive, but could see neither pointer nor figures in the smother of water. I must use the revolution-indicator. If the revs increased, the dive was becoming steeper. I must find the water surface. I dared not try to climb blind. One heavier bump to throw the seaplane into a steep bank, dive, climb or turn, and I'd never be able to find out where the sea lay, without deliberately putting the plane into a spin. But there would not be height enough to get out of a spin, once in it. I sat dead-still, left shoulder against the cockpit side, and moving only my eyes—compass—bubble level—revolution indicator—vertically downwards over the cockpit edge: travelling them from one to the other as fast as I could, only touching the control stick with light finger and thumb to ease up the plane's nose when the motor revolutions increased. There was more chance of the plane keeping itself level than of my keeping it level, flying blind. Thank God it was rigged true! There would only be time to flatten out if I picked up the water exactly where I was looking for it—vertically below— and to do that I must keep the plane dead true. "Keep cool, k-e-e-p c-o-o-l!" I saw the compass needle begin travelling to the left; I pressed the left rudder the slightest amount: the needle still travelled; I moved the rudder the least bit more. If the plane once began swinging fast enough to lock the needle . . . Yet if not very gentle I should set it swinging the other way . . . The needle still travelled. My foot tapped the rudder a fraction of an inch more. The needle checked. It began swinging back. A slight tap on the other rudder. Suppose that I could not see the water at all in this? It must be a cloudburst. I felt the strain. I might as well be coming down to the sea in the dark of night. There was more likelihood of a glint from the water in the dark. I left off saying "Keep cool"; I had no further need. My nerves had come up to scratch. I was conscious that I had never flown so well in my life. A flash of exultation.

Ahhh! A dull patch of water behind the lower wing rushed up at me. I pushed the throttle. The engine only misfired; it failed to pick up. I thrust the lever wide open, as I flattened the plane out above the water. The motor spluttered; it broke into an uneven rattle, and backfired intermittently; the plane shook from its roughness. The motor had failed! I waited, tense, for the final choke and the crash. It still fired with a harsh clatter. "Now, Minerva . . . if ever . . ." The plane kept up and lumbered on. I was terribly concentrated solely on keeping the plane flying. The motor continued with an uneven, tearing noise, but it could only be a matter of seconds—even if it did not fail completely, I was bound to strike the sea. The water was only visible to a plane's length ahead where it merged into the grey wall of rain-water. The plane was flying in the centre of a hollow grey globe with nothing by which to keep level except the small patch where globe rested on sea. I had to fly level without any mark ahead to fly by. Yet I must not rise above a few feet from the surface, or the small hole of sea in the bottom of the grey globe of visibility would vanish. I must hug every wave, whether rising or falling. The plane irritably jerked its way along as I joggled the controls unceasingly. The water pouring over my goggles distorted the look of the sea; then ran on down my face and neck. Streams of it trickled down my chest, stomach and back. I could not dart a single look at compass or any instrument: it was obvious suicide to take my eyes off the water for so long as an instant. Only one circumstance was in my favour—the very violence of the gale. Although the plane pointed in one direction, it was blown half-left, so that the next wave to be surmounted was visible to me instead of being hidden by the front of the fuselage, and I could steer by the 'feel' of the drift—otherwise must have wandered about aimlessly. The furious, cross sea was one vast, tumultuous upheaval. Here shooting upwards like a leaping flame to lick at the machine, there heaving to a great hummock. Sometimes the crests combed, boiling, down the slopes, sometimes they were slashed away bodily and hurled southwards till they dashed like flying-fish into the side of another watery hillock. But these tails of spume, streaking south across the wave valleys, enabled me to steer a straight course. I knew I was flying as I had never flown before. The vitality of every nerve seemed to have doubled. But I could not last long at the pace. Every moment I expected some muscle to lag, the plane to strike a summit and somersault into the next. Suddenly, I found myself flying straight into the water and snatched back the stick to jump the plane's nose up, thinking eye and hand had at last failed me under the strain. But at once I realized that the visibility had increased while the plane was in the trough between two rollers, and the rainfall easing had unshrouded the crest of the swell ahead and above me. Next instant the plane shot into the open air. I rose thirty feet and snatched the goggles up to my forehead. It seemed like 3,000 feet.

I had flown into a strange, unnatural stillness, as if into

the dead core of a typhoon. There was not a breath of wind, nor a drop of rain. Flitting from roller to roller, I could scarcely believe I was not in a dream. Although the waves still piled up high in pyramids or pinnacles till their summits tumbled down in ruins, they might have been of solid ice for the amazing clarity with which every line and curve, fold and shade, of every wave was limned in my brain. It gave me an impression of dead, still life. I rose to 100 feet and tore off my scarf; the wind playing down my neck soothed and some-what cooled the slow fire burning under my skin. The aneroid altimeter caught my eye; it read 900 instead of 100 feet: so the barometric pressure had dropped an inch in the last few miles. The motor! I tried the bad magneto. This time there was no drop in the revs. Good! It had recovered. Yet, strange, with the motor still running so foully. I tried the good magneto, switching off the bad.

A ghastly silence followed. The propeller still beat the air with a dead 'whirr, whirr, whirr'; but, had I woken up to find myself buried alive, the grave could not have seemed more terribly silent to me. For an instant, the blood stopped flowing in my veins, then suddenly released, it rushed through in hot flood. I switched on the remaining magneto again.* But if the water had killed one, I could expect the other, already half-dead, to follow suit at any moment. Someone had told me that I should die in my bed at eighty. The thought produced the beginning of a smile. There was a violent bump in the air; the motor fired like a chain rattling through a hawse-pipe. Next instant the plane hit another wall of grey water and immediately plunged me into blind flying. But at least I had a clear impression of the exact lie of the sea below. I at once dived the plane down steeply to the

*The sea-water had eaten through the small spring in the contact switch of one magneto and vibration or a bump had earthed the current. The other magneto was faulty because the distributor was cracked across.

144

surface and the fury of the gale and deluge had again swallowed up the plane. I felt deathly cold to the bone; it had struck into my spirit also. I was being driven till I gave up my number, cruelly, inexorably. And God! I couldn't stand this any longer. Never to stop skimming the teeth of the waves in endless jerks. I was tired to death of it. And in any case, I was bound to make the few inches' mistake sooner or later. Why not chuck it up now? A man had to die some time, in any case.

The Death of Amundsen

ROBERT DE LA CROIX

In 1926 the great polar explorer Roald Amundsen, together with the American Lincoln Ellsworth, made a flight over the North Pole by airship piloted by Umberto Nobile, a few days, incidentally, after Commander Byrd had done so by aeroplane. Subsequently Amundsen and Nobile quarrelled, largely owing to the Italian's vanity, and in 1928 Nobile mounted his own polar flight in the airship Italia. The voyage ended in disaster and Amundsen, in spite of past rancour, unhesitatingly led the rescue attempt—and was himself lost.

The first stage of the journey was to end at Stolp in Pomerania, but the *Italia* was almost wrecked on the way. Over Czechoslovakia she ran into a violent electric storm; lightning licked and played around her and she rolled and dipped in the gale, almost out of control. On one occasion the earth rushed up to meet her and it seemed as though she must crash, but with a sudden movement of the rudder Nobile succeeded in regaining height. In the end the airship weathered the storm, and on the morning of 16th April she arrived safely and only slightly damaged at her first stop. After a fortnight's stay in Germany, including an overhaul, she set off again and arrived without incident in Spitzbergen.

Time was growing short and the period of mists was approaching, but after two preliminary flights, Nobile still hesitated to give the signal for the final departure.

"Perhaps it would be better to postpone the flight until the autumn," he said.

"As far as I'm concerned that's out of the question," said Malmgren. "I must be back in Sweden by the beginning of August, and I shan't be able to go with you later."

That made up Nobile's mind—despite his desire for an all-Italian expedition, he knew that it would be dangerous to go without Malmgren, who was the only man on board with any real experience of polar exploration; so, as the meteorological report on 22nd May was on the whole favourable, he decided to start the next day.

Early on the morning of 23rd May everything was ready. It only remained for Nobile to give the order to start. The chaplain gave the airship his blessing, the three motors began to roar, Umberto Nobile issued his orders and at 4.38 a.m. the *Italia* set out on her voyage to the North Pole, amidst the cheers of 150 people who had gathered to see the start.

The wireless of the *Italia* worked efficiently, and the W/T men on board the *Citta di Milano* and throughout the world were enabled to follow the progress of the airship at regular intervals. The distance between Spitzbergen and the Pole was steadily covered: 200 miles to go; 150 miles to go; 100 miles to go . . . .

When only sixty miles from the Pole, Nobile found himself faced with an impressive barrier of black clouds. He hesitated, doubting his chances of getting through safely. Should he order the *Italia* to turn about? He was half-inclined to do so; but on the other hand it seemed a tragedy to give up so close to his objective. He decided to press on and the *Italia* sailed towards the clouds. Half an hour later she was engulfed.

At midnight the clouds cleared and the sun appeared. Zappi, Mariano, and Viglieri turned to their sextants. The latitude of the *Italia* was now 89.30 degrees. At her present rate of progress she would be over the Pole in twenty minutes. The motors kept up their steady roar.

"We are going to triumph," shouted Nobile, who had by this time given up all thought of turning back. No one spoke. The crew stared at the three officers still making their observations and scribbling feverish calculations on their pads.

"Well?" asked Nobile anxiously.

"Latitude 90 degrees," they replied simply.

Everyone rushed to the portholes to look out. The North Pole! Was it really possible that there below them was that mysterious, almost legendary point, the centre of that vast, white space on the globe, the cynosure of the polar explorers of the northern hemisphere for the past three hundred years? Yes, there spread out below them was the North Pole, a white, silent mass of drift ice on the surface of the ocean.

To tell the truth the eager watchers felt a little disappointed: the terrain they scanned so eagerly was in no way different from what they had seen on the way. The South Pole was more impressive by far. On its 10,000-feet mountain, a man could really have the impression that he was standing on top of the world. But this flat, featureless expanse failed to excite the imagination.

The *Italia* began to circle round the Pole whilst in the main cabin the Italian national anthem sounded on a gramophone, and Nobile handed round egg-punch to his crew and his companions. He was elated now. All his depression and his anxiety at the sight of that vast barrier of black cloud had gone. He had succeeded. He had shown the world that an Italian airship with an Italian commander and an Italian crew could easily do what the Americans, or the Norwegians, or any other people in the world, could do. Enthusiastically he embraced his comrades amidst cheers and joyful laughter and the excited yappings of his fox-terrier, Titine. They were all overjoyed at their success, and they shouted aloud in their triumph and danced around in glee.

Nobile had succeeded in reaching the North Pole on his own and without Amundsen's assistance, but his triumph would not be as complete as he had planned. He had wanted to do better than Amundsen: not merely to fly over the Pole, but actually descend on the ice, thanks to a specially-prepared, pneumatic-bottomed gondola and land a party to make soundings and take measurements, but owing to the mist that would now be impossible.

However, what did that matter after all? The main thing was that they had reached the Pole. "Make your observations from here," he said, and ordered the cross Pope Pius had given him to be made ready, together with an Italian flag. The *Italia* then descended to about 400 feet and Nobile let the flag and the cross fall. The cross plunged into a heap of snow.

The motors of the *Italia* were at rest in the tremendous silence of the pole, a terrible and impressive silence that most of its occupants had never encountered before. It seemed to press in on them as the mist pressed in on the *Italia* as though to crush it. The only sounds were the soughing of the wind in the stabilizers and the steady hum of the small electric dynamo.

Nobile continued to lean out of the gondola and stare down, as though fascinated, at the two dark spots which marked where the flag and the cross had fallen. He was still thinking of the words Malmgren had spoken to him only a few minutes before—

"It isn't given to many men to boast that they've been to the North Pole twice."

In fact there were only seven men in the whole world

who could say as much: a Swede, Malmgren, and six Italians, including himself, Umberto Nobile. And each time they had been taken there by an Italian airship, an airship constructed by him, Umberto Nobile.

Triumphant messages were sent out to the Pope, to King Victor Emmanuel and to the Duce, then Nobile had the motors restarted and at 02.20 he set a southward course.

Hardly had the *Italia* left the Pole when the mist closed in completely again and never lifted thereafter. Not only was there endless mist, but a strong wind from the west which reduced their speed and hampered their progress. The sun had completely disappeared and the *Italia* was now flying in darkness as deep as night. She had already been driven eastward off her course, and twenty-four hours after they had turned away from the Pole, Nobile was no longer quite sure where they were. Thanks to the directional wireless of the *Citta di Milano* he had at least a line on his position, but at what point along that line the *Italia* was situated he did not know.

Their previous exaltation had now given way to silent depression, and the crew tried to become absorbed in their work or to sleep away the time, anything to avoid thinking. Obscurely they felt that they were now to pay the price of their triumph. The *Italia* was slowing down.

"Go faster," said Malmgren to the anxious Nobile. "We must get out of this storm zone at all costs."

In answer to Nobile's orders the pitch of the motors rose and they were now doing almost forty m.p.h. but the *Italia* was still in the grip of the storm, being buffeted so violently by gusts of wind that sometimes she was driven as much as 30 degrees off her course before she could be righted. Nobile stayed at the look-out, his eyes glued to the grey space ahead and all around. According to their estimated position, he ought to be able to distinguish the outlines of the north coast of Spitzbergen by now, but he could see nothing, absolutely nothing. He was beginning to feel helpless, a prisoner of his success, of this storm, of the mist, of the ice below, even of his companions and himself.

He turned away from the porthole and looked around at the familiar interior of the gondola, at the men who stood there with him, at the picture of his little daughter Maria. He shuddered: for a moment the child's eyes had seemed full of tears.

At King's Bay the W/T men of the *Citta di Milano* sat at their instrument with the receivers round their heads. They were picking up more and more urgent demands from the *Italia* to be given her position. It was a bad sign, suggesting that Nobile had lost his way. The *Citta di Milano* continued to send out directional signals. Then, suddenly, all wireless contact with the *Italia* was lost.

They don't need us any more, the W/T men thought, taking it as a good sign. They continued to send out messages, but they received none, and they were convinced that before long the *Italia* would be sighted flying into King's Bay. The ground crew of the *Italia* made the landing-mast ready and then settled down to wait. Within two or three hours at most the silver shape of the *Italia* must appear.

But three hours passed and nothing happened. They began to grow anxious. Towards evening there was still no sign of the *Italia* and no message had been received from her. The W/T men went on sending their messages and asking for a reply, but there was none. What was the matter with Nobile? At least he might give some sign of life to ease the mounting tension.

As the light failed, so the fear that an accident might have happened developed into a reluctant conviction. Wireless apparatus could get out of order, of course, but in the worst case an hour or two ought to suffice to put it in order.

Unless the wireless apparatus had been destroyed. But that would probably mean that the *Italia* had been destroyed too. Had the elements got the better of her at last?

The *Italia* had enough fuel-oil on board for a ninety-hour flight; so much was known for certain. By the early morning of 27th May, therefore, it became quite clear that she could no longer be flying—at least, not under control. At the best she might still be in the air, but as a mere drifting gas-bag at the mercy of wind and weather. But where? No sign of her had been seen anywhere near Spitzbergen. Had the wind carried her towards Iceland, or out to the open sea?

On 29th May an American newspaper published a sensational report to the effect that she had landed in Alaska. Inquiries made immediately by the U.S. authorities proved the report to be a canard. On 30th May seal-hunters reported that they had seen distress signals on Amsterdam Island, to the north of Spitzbergen. It was confidently believed that the signals must come from Nobile, but a vessel dispatched to the spot found nothing. The seal-hunters must have been misled, probably by the Arctic lights.

The Norwegian authorities warned the public against false reports and proposed to all the countries directly concerned in the question that they should co-operate in a large-scale search. But on 31st May a request was received from the Italian Fascist Government that this proposal should for the time being, at least, not be followed up. The Norwegians were puzzled. The Italian Government had first asked for assistance. Why were they no longer anxious to receive it? The lives of brave men were in danger. Were the Italians nationalistic enough to be influenced by the unimportant squabbles of two years ago? Did they perhaps think that it would be beneath their dignity to accept assistance from Norwegians?

Amundsen, who had already agreed unhesitatingly to lead the rescue-search for the airship, was consulted on the point.

"The thing's silly," he said tersely. "Whatever they think, we must be above considerations of that sort." And he turned at once to the practical details of the rescue. "The main difficulty at this season is that drift ice makes navigation very hazardous, north of Spitzbergen."

But what concerned him most of all was that for the moment he had no means of setting out on the rescue-attempt. The search required a plane with a big radius of action, and unfortunately his friend the American Ellsworth, who had flown with him in the *Norge*, had not yet answered a cable he had sent.

Amundsen was very disturbed at the situation. As a veteran polar explorer, he knew how very real the dangers were. In contrast, the Italian Press, not burdened by any expert knowledge, showed astonishing and quite unfounded optimism. The *Stampa* was typical of all other newspapers in a country whose Press was closely controlled. "That crystal-like and unshakable courage which has supported our airmen up to now will not forsake them, and we firmly believe that before long we shall hear great and glorious news from the distant seas of ice."

At that Amundsen could only shrug his shoulders. He hoped for good news too, but the harsh fact remained that all the regular wireless stations, including the most modern and powerful, as well as hundreds of amateur short-wave wireless enthusiasts, were all striving to pick up messages from the *Italia* on the agreed 33-metre wavelength, but without success. Here, too, there were, of course, various reports: fragments of an appeal were said to have been picked up, but it had not been possible to identify the sender with any certainty. And if they had actually come from Nobile how was it possible to explain that the W/T men of the *Citta di Milano* had heard nothing?

The listening on the Italian base-ship was organized systematically and with the utmost possible care: at the fifty-fifth minute of every other hour (even hours) as previously arranged, the W/T men of the *Citta di Milano* were sitting at their panels with earphones on, straining to catch the slightest crackle that might be a dot or a dash. But at the end of each agreed period they would take off their earphones and put them down with a gesture of disappointment. Nothing. Absolutely nothing . . .

A short-wave wireless amateur in Altoona, Pennsylvania, reported that he had received a message:

SOS. No shelter except wreckage of airship. Position: Latitude 84 degrees 15' 06" north; longitude 15 degrees 02' east.

But on the face of it this looked like a hoax. At the time of the supposed accident the *Italia* must have been somewhere in the neighbourhood of latitude 80. How could she possibly have drifted so far north?

At the beginning of June the newspapers were unanimous in believing that the *Italia* and her crew were definitely lost. The photographs of the leading men of the expedition were published; the preparations for the flight were criticized and even its utility was called into question. Only the Italian Press, under orders, continued to present a brave front of optimism, declaring with assumed confidence that the explorers would soon return in triumph.

The world Press did not share this manufactured optimism, and it recalled an observation made by Amundsen the previous year during the unfortunate squabble with Nobile. Referring to the times when the *Norge* had almost crashed, Amundsen had declared, "Had he really crashed on the ice, he would have had very little hope of ever seeing a civilized country again."

The Death of Amundsen

All experienced polar explorers knew that Amundsen had been speaking the simple truth: a long march over drift ice demanded not only nerves of steel and physical resistance of a high order, but also long experience of Arctic conditions, if it were not to end in disaster. Apart from the Swede, Malmgren, not a single member of the Nobile expedition possessed any experience at all. In the circumstances the chances of survival of any men who might have escaped the supposed crash were very problematical. Nothing whatever had been heard for ten days now. All reports of messages received had been carefully examined, and they had all proved to be either honest errors or deliberate hoaxes. It required a good deal of optimism to believe that there was still any hope for the *Italia* and her crew.

World opinion was so convinced that Nobile and his companions were lost that when, on 4th June, the Soviet Government informed the Italian Ambassador to Moscow that a wireless amateur named Schmitt had received a message that seemed to come from Nobile, people were inclined to believe that it was another false alarm.

But this time they were wrong. Schmitt, a keen amateur who had built himself a short-wave set to occupy his leisure hours in a God-forsaken part of Russia near Archangel, really *had* picked up a message. It was a puzzling communication, but on the whole that seemed to speak in favour of its authenticity. All the other messages invented by practical jokers had given too many precise details, which was hardly plausible for men lost on the ice from a much-buffeted airship whose commander had lost his way. The message Schmitt claimed to have heard read simply: *"Italian Nobile Franz Joseph S.O.S. S.O.S. Terra tengo E.h.H."*

Whilst the experts went into a huddle over this singular assortment of letters the wireless appeals were reported to be continuing. They were weak and they were often incomprehensible, but they were still coming in from somewhere. Most people doubted their authenticity.

"We've nearly been caught more than once," said Captain Romagna of the *Citta di Milano*. "We must keep our heads and wait patiently."

The airman Lutzow Holm arrived at Spitzbergen with two ships, the *Braganza* and the *Hobby*.

"Wait?" he demanded. "What for? Until they die one by one?" and he flew off in his plane towards North East Land and disappeared.

"It was madness," exclaimed Romagna. "I told you so. We need reliable information if we are to do anything worth while."

To test the authenticity of the messages, he got the idea of asking the sender for the number of Biagi's registration certificate. Biagi was the chief wireless operator of the *Italia*. No hoaxer would have that information. The unknown sender gave his number. It was checked and found to be correct. It was true! The messages received by the Soviet wireless amateur Schmitt were coming from Nobile's expedition!

The Italian Press went into ecstasies—

"They live! They breathe! They speak! It was their faith and ours—still unshakeable—that protected them. And tomorrow—as is the dearest wish of all our hearts—it will bring them back to us, victorious! Our heroes now expect other heroes to brave the distance and the elements to join them and give them back, covered with glory, to the bosom of Mother Italy."

Despite these fine-sounding words Nobile and his comrades were far from being saved yet. The drama of the *Italia* was not at an end; it was only just beginning. Those "other heroes" were quite ready to "brave the distance and the elements" and they were even now preparing to do so, studying their maps and charts, tuning up their engines and getting ready for the venture which might well cost them their own lives. But as for their success, that was still by no means certain.

On 25th May, in the morning, the *Italia* was flying south blindly when a shout came—"The elevators are jammed!"

It was 09.25 and the airship began to lose height. The cold white stretch of ice below seemed to rise up to meet them. Nobile ordered the motors to be switched off, but despite this precaution the *Italia* still fell rapidly. She was no more than five hundred feet up now, and through the portholes her crew could already distinguish the features of the ice field rising towards them. At three hundred feet it was possible to calculate on which jagged crest of ice the *Italia* would be ripped to pieces. At 150 feet, someone shouted suddenly, "We've stopped falling!"

It was not quite true, but the rate of falling had decreased and at 100 feet the *Italia* began to rise again. Nobile heaved a sigh of relief and brought her up to about 3,000 feet, well above the mist. Whilst the mechanics looked for the trouble, the navigational officers took the *Italia*'s position from the sun. Nobile was in a quandary: it would certainly be very much more agreeable to fly at height and stay above the mist, and certainly less immediately dangerous. On the other hand there was the risk that they would fly even further off their course, which they could certainly not afford to do. By this time there was barely enough fuel oil left to get them back to their mooring-mast. If they flew low, however, they would at least be able to observe the drift. Rather hesitantly, Nobile decided that to fly low was the lesser of the two evils.

Once again the all-pervading mist closed in, but below them they could see the drift ice. The mechanics had got the elevators in order and Nobile felt reasonably safe again. The airship's speed increased and for a while everything seemed to be going well. But then there was another shout—"She's out of trim!"

It was true. The *Italia* dipped her tail sharply and began to lose height rapidly, sagging down towards the ice, tail first. This time it seemed inevitable that she must crash.

"Increase speed. Start up the third engine," ordered Nobile. Anxiously he studied the variometer. She ought to start rising—or at least stop falling. No, the rapid descent was uninterrupted. Nobile continued to stare at the instrument. His face was very white now. He knew that the final crash was a matter of seconds, and there was nothing he could do to prevent it.

Everyone on board realized the situation, but there was no panic, just a cold fear that froze their hearts whilst their bodies continued mechanically to make whatever movements were necessary. The men's faces were rigid as they waited for the crash. Nobile seized the helm. Perhaps at least he could guide the *Italia* so that in her fall she ploughed into a snowdrift rather than ripped herself up on the jagged ice. The ice could be seen very clearly now: every crevasse, every jagged point, every cruel ridge.

Another sixty feet . . . thirty feet . . . "Let it be quick!" prayed the men. "Let it be quick!" They expected a hard jolt, but when it came it was a tremendous smash that seemed to split everything apart in one vast roar of sound . . .

Nobile lay helplessly on the ice. His right leg and his right arm were broken, and he felt as though something in his head were bursting, whilst a fire consumed his lungs. The first shock was wearing off and he was rapidly becoming conscious of increasing pain.

He opened his eyes, and the first thing he saw was the *Italia*. She was in the air again with her tail dragging low as she drifted quickly towards the east. Her envelope was slack and creased now, but at least she had height. Cables, or perhaps spars—he was unable to see very well—were hanging from her. One thing was quite clearly discernible: the great letters along her side which spelt *Italia*, a name which now seemed sinister, a harbinger of evil and suffering.

Incredulously he stared at the receding airship. What had happened? How was it possible for the *Italia* to be sailing away in the distance, leaving her commander here helplessly on the ice? Was he dreaming? Or was he already dead?

He moved a little and pain shot through his broken limbs. He groaned, and he heard someone else groan near him. Then he saw a heap of wreckage and scattered objects on the ice around him. Some of his companions were there too— Ceccioni, Mariano, Trojani, with blood running down his face, Behounek the Czech, Malmgren the Swede and Viglieri. And already on their feet were Zappi and Biagi, the wireless operator. Mariano was asking weakly, "Where is the General? Where is the General?"

Nobile stared again at the receding airship, disappearing into the mist. All that was still clearly visible was the name *Italia*, and on the ice in the direction in which she was drifting were glaring patches of red from falling bottles of aniline dye, used for judging altitude. It was like a long line of blood splashes to mark the trail of the *Italia* as she was swept away by the wind—with eight men on board.

From the debris of steel spars, torn envelope and matchwood around him, Nobile realized what had happened. The violent shock as the airship hit the ice had torn away the main gondola in which he and the others around him had been at the time. Lightened by its loss, the *Italia* had then leapt into the air again and continued her course, taking with her the eight men in the other gondola.

The survivors stared silently after their ship. Gradually

159

their thankfulness at being still alive gave way to a realization of their position; they had no food, no shelter and no wireless apparatus with which they could let the world know of their plight. As far as Nobile could judge, they were about a month's march across the ice to the nearest land. He called the roll. One man had been killed in the crash. It was Pomella. His dead body lay a little to one side.

"I envy him," said Nobile. "He was luckier than we were. He was granted the blessing of a quick death."

Nine men were still alive apart from the eight in the *Italia*. There seemed no hope for any of them. All they could look forward to was a slow and miserable death from cold and starvation.

Convinced that they must all die, Nobile closed his eyes and lay there where the others had covered him up. In the meantime, the still able-bodied men began to search through the wreckage to see what they could find. There was a tent, warm clothing, some signal rockets and a variety of oddments, some of them damaged.

Suddenly there was a wild shout from Biagi. He had found a portable wireless set. Hurriedly he examined it. It was complete and, as far as he could see, intact. With trembling fingers he checked the connections, the dial and the accumulators. It worked! Hastily they set up an aerial, and he prepared to transmit. He was overjoyed. He could imagine the sensation his first message would create when it was received by the *Citta di Milano* in Spitzbergen. Nobile, no longer thinking of death, dictated an appeal for assistance. A man of mercurial temperament, his thoughts were now all on their rescue.

Having sent off the message Biagi settled down to listen for the reply. It came:

Italia keep up your courage. We are coming to your assistance.

The message came from the *Citta di Milano*.

160

Biagi listened anxiously for details of the promised rescue operations. The same message was repeated:

Italia keep up your courage. We are coming to your assistance.

When it came through the third time Biagi began to look puzzled. Had they heard him correctly? He sent out his message again, adding: *Have you understood?* Then he listened despondently.

Italia keep up your courage. We are coming to your assistance, said the *Citta di Milano.*

"I don't believe they've heard us at all," Biagi declared with disappointment. "They keep sending out the same thing again and again. There's no reference to receiving my message."

He sent it out again, and again came the stereotyped words from the Italian ship.

"They're not receiving us!" he exclaimed in despair. "They haven't heard a thing."

He tried again. Again the same result. At intervals *Citta di Milano* sent out the same empty message.

"It's enough to drive a man mad," he declared. "Why can't they hear us?"

He began sending again: *S.O.S. Italia, near Foyn Island. Our position at the moment . . . .*

Every other hour at the agreed time he sent out his messages, and all he heard in return was the same mechanical phrase *Italia keep up your courage . . .*

That evening, messages picked up from European stations confirmed his conviction that their messages were not being received: *Although wireless watch has been systematically organized, no message of any sort has been received from the Italia . . .*

"I can't understand it," shouted Biagi in rage and mortification. "Why can't anyone hear us? They ought to hear us." And doggedly he set to work again: *S.O.S. Italia . . .*

But all he heard from Europe was: *The absolute silence on the air compels us to fear the worst* . . . And the gist of this was repeated in half a dozen languages.

We are on drift ice, persisted Biagi. *Our position is changing constantly. We need food, clothing, accumulators. Our position at the moment* . . .

But what came back to him was: *Why is nothing whatever heard from the Italia or from possible survivors? We hardly dare answer that agonizing question. Can we still reasonably hope that anyone is still alive?*

For perhaps the hundredth time, almost weeping with rage, Biagi checked his apparatus. The needle of the ammeter showed that the sender was in order.

"Why don't they hear us?" he demanded. "I can't understand it, I tell you. They must hear us."

His companions looked at him with consternation. What sort of a nightmare was this, on top of their already desperate situation?

"If they can't hear us now there'll be less and less chance of their hearing us later, because the accumulators will run down," declared Biagi grimly. "The power's already less than it was."

It began to look as though the joyful discovery of the intact wireless apparatus had been a bitter trick played on them by fate, to raise their spirits before they were crushed for good and all.

And in the meantime, plaints continued to come from all European stations: *Why don't they give some sign of wireless life? For eleven days now nothing has been heard from the Italia* . . .

It was clear that back in Europe people believed them dead. This mental torture, added to their plight, lasted for eleven days and then on 6th June, Biagi, who was jotting down the Italian news sent out by a short-wave station in Sao Paolo, began to show signs of excitement as he scribbled feverishly.

"We've been heard at last!" he shouted when he put down his earphones. "Some Russian amateur . . . His government has informed our Ambassador in Moscow . . ."

The others crowded round him and the two wounded men, Nobile and Ceccioni, crawled over. All eyes were shining with renewed hope, though they hardly dared believe.

"But I'm quite sure," insisted Biagi. "There's no doubt about it. I can't have been dreaming. Here it is." And he handed his pad to Nobile, who read it in silence and then appeared to be studying it.

"Is there anything you can't understand in it, General?" Biagi finally demanded.

"Yes, there is," said Nobile slowly. "It's odd, but this isn't the text of the message you sent out. My message began *S.O.S. Italia, near Foyn Island* . . . But this message talks about *Franz Josef Land.* If they take any notice of that it means they'll search much too far east."

It was maddening. Fate seemed against them.

"Send out a correction, Biagi. Do it right now."

Whilst Biagi was sending out the new message, Nobile studied the one that had been repeated to them from Sao Paolo, trying to solve this new mystery which had arisen to plague them.

"I think I've got it," he said finally. "There's probably been some confusion in the reception between '*circa*' and '*Foyn*'. They seem to have made Francesco out of it."

Then on June 8 the wireless of the *Citta di Milano* acknowledged receipt of their new message. At last they had got things straight; now the rescue work could begin in earnest.

In the meantime, three of the survivors, the two Italian naval officers Zappi and Mariano, and the Swedish scientist Malmgren, had set off for land on foot. As yet nothing had been heard of them.

When the first halting messages from Nobile were picked up —they sounded rather like the incoherent mutterings of a very sick man—it was immediately supposed that the wireless apparatus had been so seriously damaged in the crash that it had taken over a week to repair. Now the world learned with stupefaction that although the first coherent conversation had taken place on 8th June the Nobile group had begun sending messages on 25th May, a few hours after the crash. Another remarkable and inexplicable thing was that now, although the batteries of the small apparatus Biagi was using were running down, the *Citta di Milano* was receiving his messages quite clearly.

For some reason or other the Italians first concealed part of the truth. For example on 10th June the *Citta di Milano* announced that all the members of the expedition were safe. The following day it announced that the *Italia* has been completely destroyed and that two members of the crew had been injured. The day after that, 12th June, it announced that the *Italia* had disappeared with half the crew on board, and that Nobile and those with him must be on drift ice, because their position was changing daily.

This news caused consternation amongst the would-be rescuers. What they had at first thought to be good news now turned out to be tragic news. A group of men with Nobile at their head were still alive! So far so good . . . But how were they to be rescued? Without sledges and without skis it was quite impossible for them to make land on their own, particularly carrying injured men. No aeroplane could possibly land and take off on the chaotic terrain offered by drift ice. So what could be done for the survivors?

Everyone turned to Amundsen. It was impossible to do anything without him, without his advice, without the benefit of his vast polar experience.

"The *Italia* survivors are in a very dangerous position,"

he declared. "The polar drift is steadily carrying them away. What we need to help them is either the big hydroplane I have already asked for, or an ice-breaker."

And that summed up the situation. What Amundsen said could be taken as gospel, for no man knew better than he did. One or the other of the things he proposed must be tried—or both. And as quickly as possible. The situation was urgent.

Unfortunately the American had not replied to Amundsen and so there was no hydroplane available. There were three aeroplanes at Spitzbergen: Lutzow Holm's plane—fortunately he had turned up again; Riiser Larsen's plane; and the plane of the Italian Maddalena. They had already made extensive flights without finding any trace of Nobile's tent, which was red in order to facilitate observation from the air. No doubt one or the other of them would find the group in the end and then the most urgent supplies could be dropped. That would help, but it would not be the final solution of the problem: the men couldn't be taken off. For that purpose, a plane would have to land and take off again and that was impossible in such terrain.

As far as Amundsen's second proposal—an ice-breaker— was concerned, a Soviet rescue committee had already been formed to study ways and means of helping the marooned Italians, and it wasted no time. On 16th June ships in the Baltic encountered a curiously built vessel with two long black funnels, a strangely rounded hull and hatchet-like bows. The wind was not very strong, but it was enough to make this odd vessel pitch and roll heavily as it ploughed its way through the water. Its progress was laborious, painfully so, but that was because it had not been designed for open waters. Through ice-floes, however, its progress was spectacular. Thanks to its two specially designed screws and to the rapid filling and emptying of its fore and aft ballast tanks—a process which gave it a strange up and down movement—it

165

could forge its way through ice. This strange vessel was the *Leonid Krassin*, the biggest and most powerful ice-breaker in the world, and she was on her way to the rescue of the survivors of the *Italia*.

The departure of the Soviet ice-breaker the day before had aroused little interest in the world Press because just at that moment its chief interest was centred on Roald Amundsen, who had at last obtained the big hydroplane he wanted. It was not from Ellsworth, who had still not replied, but from the French Government. When the *Italia* disaster occurred, this plane was undergoing its trials before making an attempt on the world long-distance, straight-line flight record, first to Jibuti and then across the Atlantic. It carried a crew of four: Guilbaud the pilot, Cuverville the navigator, Vallette the mechanic and Brazy the wireless operator.

Amundsen had weighed up the pros and cons very carefully. He, if anyone, was fully aware of the dangers involved, but he was confident that with a little luck he could succeed. He had fought both Poles with their snow, their ice, their mists and their intense cold for thirty-five years and in that time he had become a hardened veteran, acknowledged by the world as one of its greatest explorers. From the age of eighteen he had followed his chosen career with grim determination. He had gone through a good deal in that time, enduring physical sufferings and bitter disappointments. One thing he had acquired to the point of second nature: a sense of human solidarity. He knew that he could have done nothing on his own, that he owed much of his success to the many comrades, some of them unknown to the world, who had supported him. A good deal of the glory the world had accorded him belonged in reality to them. So when the offer of the French Government reached him in his little house, where he lived quite alone without even a servant, he did not hesitate for a moment.

Nobile had been unfair and irritating, but they had flown over the North Pole together. Despite their differences they were comrades-in-arms against the ice. Amundsen knew more or less where Nobile was now and his position was unenviable. Seal-hunters, men inured to tough conditions, called it "the white hell". The man needed help, and he must have it as quickly as possible if he and his comrades were to survive. And then, Amundsen had the feeling that the Pole, once defeated by him, was challenging him again through Nobile. "I've got him," it seemed to say. "Come and get him—if you can, and dare."

Amundsen wasn't the sort of man to evade any challenge. The corners of his mouth turned up in a grim little smile. If he dared? He'd dare all right. He studied the latest information he had received. Guilbaud was already on his way to Bergen. From there he was to fly to Tromsö where he would take on fuel. After that he would make for King's Bay.

Why fly from Tromsö to King's Bay? Amundsen thought. Why not fly direct from Tromsö to Nobile on his ice-floe? Better still, why not try to discover the missing airship itself? After all, it wasn't by any means certain that the men on board had perished. Relieved of the weight of the main gondola, it could have risen to 10,000 feet and perhaps come down later.

Amundsen knew that Nobile had reported having seen a cloud of smoke approximately twenty miles away, about a quarter of an hour after the first crash and that he had concluded from that the *Italia* had finally crashed and caught fire. But later he had admitted that perhaps the cloud of smoke had not been dense enough to have come from a burning airship. It might even have been a distress signal from the other survivors. In the circumstances, Nobile might have fallen victim to an optical illusion, perhaps mistaking some thicker patch of mist for smoke.

As he thought it over, Amundsen came to the conclusion that, apart from the one man known to be dead, all the members of the expedition might well be still alive. He said as much to the journalists who surrounded him clamouring for a statement, and he added,

"We shall do our best to get north as quickly as possible. We shall leave nothing undone to help these men, but our progress will, of course, depend to some extent on the weather conditions we encounter."

At one o'clock in the afternoon on 16th June, the French hydroplane, a *Latham*, touched down safely in Bergen Fjord, leaving a long, white wake behind it in the diffused light of an Arctic summer, a milky glimmer made up of both dawn and twilight. That same evening Amundsen went on board, and a little after nine o'clock the *Latham* took off again and arrived safely in Tromsö early the next morning.

It was seven o'clock when Amundsen set off on his own to walk through the deserted streets of the town. He wanted to be alone to think. He knew Tromsö very well. The place was specially dear to him, because it was from here that the *Gjöa*, the *Fram* and the *Maud* had all set off on their famous expeditions, and each ship had returned here in a blaze of glory. Today, the 17th June 1928, he would set out again to snatch a group of men from an icy grave, to rescue men who, like him, had tried to defeat the ice but had themselves been defeated. Roald Amundsen thanked God that he had been given the chance of setting the crown on his career by this errand of mercy and human solidarity.

His heavy steps resounded in the empty streets. In the shop windows as he passed, he could see pictures of himself, effigies stamped on tablets of soap or printed on cigarette packets. He was tremendously popular in Norway and his fellow-countrymen idolized him. When he observed such signs he was not moved by any vanity or pride. For him this demonstration of regard was a source of strength, a further reason to believe in his mission, a heartening thing that made him feel safer and more confident. It was good and deeply satisfying to know that the strength of a whole people was behind him. He could still hear the acclamations that greeted him on his return from his expeditions; he could still smell the scent of the flowers handed to him by little children.

He paused before a book-shop window. There was his photograph, taken two years before, when he had returned in triumph from the successful expedition of the *Norge* to the North Pole. He studied it with interest. I look old with all those lines and wrinkles, he thought. And yet I was only fifty-four. The grim conditions he had experienced so often made a man look old before his time. Today he had the impression that he had already lived through two or three ordinary lives. Odd that death has never turned his attention to me, he thought. I gave him chances enough.

Musing, he walked on until he came to the shop of the chemist, Zapfe, one of his oldest friends and perhaps his closest. Like all Norwegians, Zapfe venerated him. In Zapfe's study a silhouette of Amundsen hung on the wall. Amundsen had not seen it before.

"Very touching, my dear Zapfe, but I'm becoming a bit of a fetish I'm afraid."

Zapfe smiled.

"We've got our own ideas, Roald, but get some rest now. A plane journey through the night probably wasn't very restful."

He made his visitor breakfast. Amundsen's mind was already revolving round his great task.

"Any further news?" he asked.

"Not really. Nobile's in a critical position. He says the ice around them is breaking up and big areas of sea suddenly appear without warning."

"But that's good news," said Amundsen. "It means that a hydroplane could touch down on one of those open spaces of ice-free water. Just the thing I have in mind. Given a little luck with the weather and we ought to do the trick."

After breakfast he telephoned to the Geophysical Institute, which collected and collated all reports concerning weather conditions in the Arctic Circle. They informed him that there was a bank of mist in the neighbourhood of Bear Island, half-way between North Cape and Spitzbergen. Unfortunately that was the route he was proposing to take. Never mind, they would have to get round it somehow.

"When are you leaving?" asked Zapfe.

"At four o'clock this afternoon."

"So soon!"

"How much time do you think we've got to spare?"

Amundsen looked at the morning papers. Nobile was still sending messages. There was a lot of talk, but not a great deal of action and what there was, was often ill-considered and dangerous. "Audacity's all right in its place," thought Amundsen, "but it isn't everything, by a long chalk." He looked to see what the Russians were doing. Two ice-breakers were on their way: the *Malygin* from Novaya Zemlya and the *Krassin* from Norwegian waters. "Good," he thought, "if I don't succeed, they'll be well placed to take over."

Towards four o'clock that afternoon, the time fixed for the take-off, Amundsen walked down to the harbour with his friend Zapfe. The *Latham* was moored opposite the hospital, with its nose already pointing down the fjord.

As impassible as ever, Amundsen took his place in the rear of the hydroplane, hardly acknowledging the cheers of the crowd that had gathered. The ovations even seemed to annoy him. He had done nothing as yet. When he had done the job, they could cheer their heads off if they wanted to.

Dietrichson, a specialist in polar flying, took his place

beside Amundsen. Guilbaud and Cuverville were already seated at their instrument panel. Brazy was before his wireless apparatus.

"Well, what are we waiting for?" demanded Amundsen a trifle irritably. He was tired of hearing his name shouted again and again by the enthusiastic crowds on the jetties.

"Amundsen! Amundsen! Amundsen! Good luck Amundsen!"

He made a brief salute with raised arm and then ignored the shouting and waving. First one air-screw began to turn and then the other. The roar of the motors now cut them off from the spectators, who were still shouting, still gesticulating wildly, but as though in dumb show. The hydroplane began its run down the fjord and then rose gracefully into the air. The jetties and the harbour grew smaller and smaller beneath them, the hydroplane banked and turned and then they were over the open sea. Behind them the watchers at Tromsö stared at a black speck in the sky visible just above the sea-line for a while, and then it disappeared from view.

At five o'clock the *Latham* passed Ekhingen Lighthouse. Brazy kept in regular contact with the wireless station of the Geophysical Institute. At a quarter to seven their operator broke contact with *Latham* to send out the regular meteorological reports for shipping. Such reports were of the utmost importance, particularly to fishing vessels. The lives of their crews and the success of their operations depended on them. In no circumstances could they be delayed, and, in any case, there was no need, because the *Latham* could be left to its own devices quite safely for a while. Everything was going well on board.

At eight o'clock the operator tried to resume contact:

Hallo Latham! Hallo Latham! Geophysical Institute calling. Geophysical Institute calling. Can you hear me? Report your position. Hallo Latham! Answer please. Answer please.

But there was no answer and there was to be no answer. In that short space of time, Amundsen's fate had fulfilled itself. He had laid down his life for Nobile. Norway was never to see her great son again.

You can rely on Amundsen. He is the only real expert in these matters. Go to him for advice. Get him to organize a rescue party with sledges . . .

It was Nobile talking from his ice-floe. Now that contact with the world had been securely established he was sending a constant flow of messages. He was worried by the difficulties his would-be rescuers were encountering, and he was placing his hopes above all in one man, Roald Amundsen, his enemy of yesterday. When Nobile learned that Amundsen was about to set out to search for him and his party he was overjoyed.

"He has banished not only every shadow of resentment but even the very memory of the dispute which arose between us owing to a regrettable misunderstanding." Nobile was confident now. If any man could save him, Roald Amundsen could.

But the reply he received from the *Citta di Milano* exploded like a bombshell and blasted the high confidence that the first news had created on the ice-floe:

We are unable to approach Amundsen for any further assistance because his hydroplane has been lost without trace.

Those brief words shattered Nobile. He was overcome. At first he was hardly able to credit their truth. Amundsen? Was it possible? He had already been imagining their historic meeting on the ice-floe, a scene to be immortalized for the benefit of future generations—Nobile and Amundsen reconciled. Instead of that the world would now make him in part responsible for more deaths. It was as though fate were conspiring against him.

"Amundsen can't disappear just like that," he declared incredulously. "It can't be true."

And in Norway people were saying the same thing: "Amundsen can't disappear just like that. It can't be true." They began to recover their optimism. The explanation of the affair was obvious: if the *Latham* had broken off wireless contact, it was because Amundsen had, for reasons of his own, ordered it to do so. He probably wanted to go ahead with his own plans without interference and not reveal them to the world too soon. Yes, that was it—just as he had taken no one into his confidence before his departure. There was some suggestion that he intended to search for the *Italia* first because the eight men left alive on it had sledges, provisions, clothing and everything necessary to resist even Arctic conditions and bring them back safely—provided they could be found alive and guided to safety. After that Nobile's turn would come.

But time passed inexorably, and there was still no sign from Amundsen, though each day brought new reports eagerly snapped up by optimists, only to be denied: he had touched down on the sea near Nobile; he had found the *Italia*; he had made a forced landing at Cape Leigh-Smith with engine trouble . . .

Although report after report was seen to be false, people still did not lose hope—not where Amundsen was concerned. "If there has been a forced landing, he has survived somewhere," they said confidently to each other. "After all, it's Amundsen. He'll be saved."

But by whom? The problem of saving Amundsen, if he was still to be saved, was very much like the problem of saving Nobile, which had first started the whole business. People looked anxiously to all quarters from which help might come. The situation remained as Amundsen himself had briefly summed it up: they would be saved, if at all, by a hydroplane in one swift flight—or by an ice-breaker. What were the Russians doing? The *Malygin* was still too far away to be of any practical assistance, but the most powerful ice-breaker of all, the *Krassin*, was already approaching the Arctic. On the 21st June, towards evening, it entered the calm waters of Bergen Fjord and anchored opposite the coaling-station to take on further supplies.

The news spread through the town like wildfire: "The *Krassin* has just put into harbour. It carries an aeroplane on board. The Russians will find Amundsen and bring him back."

Professor Samoilovitch, who was in charge of the Soviet rescue expedition, came ashore to get the latest news concerning Amundsen's disappearance. There were two reports. This time both of them were authentic. Fishermen had seen the *Latham* touching down in Malangen Fjord very soon after the take-off from Tromsö, no doubt to carry out some minor repair or adjustment. An hour later, a tramp had sighted a hydroplane on the sea about seventy miles from the Norwegian coast.

It looked as though Guilbaud had been having trouble with his engines. The last wireless signals from the *Latham* had been picked up towards eight o'clock. Taking the *Latham's* speed to be about a 100 m.p.h., that should have brought Amundsen and his party somewhere in the neighbourhood of Bear Island. Samoilovitch turned the matter over in his mind and decided to look for Amundsen first— but quickly, very quickly, for he had not forgotten that Nobile's situation on the ice-floe was rapidly growing desperate. As far as Amundsen was concerned, the *Krassin* would question the numerous ships which cruised around Bear Island in the summer months. Amundsen might already be on one of them in safety, together with Dietrichson and the crew of the *Latham*.

The Death of Amundsen

At dawn on 24th June the *Krassin* put to sea again. On the hillsides along the coast the fires lit to celebrate the Feast of St. John were burning low. All night long the flames had leapt up and rockets had soared into the sky to welcome Midsummer Day, the feast of the sun, the feast of life itself. Soon the *Krassin* left the glowing embers behind and the shouts which accompanied her out of harbour—"Bring Amundsen back! Bring Amundsen back!" The Russian sailors on deck had not understood the meaning of those shouts, and they had replied cheerfully with waves of the hand and much good-natured laughter.

But Professor Samoilovitch knew what they meant. He paced the bridge of the *Krassin* as they sailed along the coast of Bear Island. The island shores were invisible in a great bank of mist, but its summit jutted out into the clearer air above. All around, curtains of mist swung back and closed again constantly, in a sort of lugubrious ballet of the air. As she went forward the *Krassin* sounded her siren in long, hoarse bellowings. The watch was reinforced and the men did their best to penetrate the all-pervading mist, but it was quite hopeless. There was no chance of seeing a thing. The Russian sailors, who knew now what the Norwegians had shouted to them, were oppressed by the thought that below the thrashing screws of their vessel six bodies were probably being buffeted here and there by the waves.

By 30th June the *Krassin* had left Spitzbergen far behind and was crushing her way through the first fields of ice. The quest for Amundsen had proved vain, and Professor Samoilovitch was hoping that they would have better luck with Nobile. On that day the wireless operator of the *Krassin* came up to him with a message he had just received. Samoilovitch read it and shook his head in astonishment at its contents.

It was from General Nobile, who, already in safety, now requested to be allowed to accompany the *Krassin* on her voyage to save his marooned comrades. How was it possible that the leader of the expedition was in safety whilst his men were still in danger? Samoilovitch even began to wonder whether the message was a hoax.

It was not. Nobile was safe and his men were still on the ice-floe. The circumstances in which he had left them were never explained altogether to the satisfaction of the world, and the incident contributed to thickening the clouds of doubt and suspicion which were beginning to gather ominously around the ill-starred expedition of the *Italia*.

When Samoilovitch received that astonishing telegram, Nobile had already been four days on board the *Citta di Milano*. Of all those men who had been in danger for a month now, he was the only man in safety. Others had not been so fortunate.

The eight men still on board the *Italia* when she regained height and was blown away were presumably lost. Amundsen, Guilbaud, Dietrichson, Brazy, Cuverville and Vallette were also lost. The Italian skier and his guide Van Dongen, who had set out over the ice from Spitzbergen were missing, presumed lost. Two airmen who had set out from the deck of the ice-breaker *Malygin* on a reconnaissance flight had failed to return to their ship and were feared lost. And, finally, nothing had been heard of the group consisting of the two Italian naval officers Zappi and Mariano and the Swede Malmgren, who had set out from Nobile's ice-floe in an attempt to reach land on their own.

Those who had stayed behind with Nobile on the ice-floe were still alive, but they were in danger, and as the ice-floe steadily drifted further and further away, their situation was becoming more and more precarious. The group had a new member now: the Swedish airman Lundborg. With a small plane fitted with skis he had taken off Nobile, but crashed on his second journey. He was now a prisoner on the ice-floe together with the others.

Fortunately there was the *Krassin* with a real chance of rescuing the marooned group, and now the whole world anxiously followed the ice-breaker's northward progress. Owing to the ice she advanced with nerve-racking slowness, steaming forward to break the ice, steaming backwards to give herself a new run for the next attempt. On 3rd July her progress ceased altogether. "The *Krassin* no longer answers satisfactorily to her helm," reported Samoilovitch. "One blade of her starboard screw is broken."

When Nobile heard the news on board the *Citta di Milano* he broke down; he felt that fate was against him and against all those who had come to his assistance. He was a prisoner in his cabin on Mussolini's orders, and the biggest ice-breaker in the world, on which they had all set such hopes, was now still and silent amidst the ice with only a wisp or two of smoke curling from her two tall funnels.

He re-lived the nightmare of the past, with its hopes and fears. The position of the little red tent had at last been spotted from the air and supplies had been safely dropped: food, clothing, collapsible boats and arms. Rescue had begun to look very near. Under his orders the men had succeeded in making a small runway on the ice, too small unfortunately, and none of the flyers had been prepared to risk their machines on it until Lundborg had arrived with the one aeroplane provided with skis. He had touched down safely—"Like an archangel from heaven," Nobile had noted enthusiastically.

"I am taking the injured men first," Lundborg had said. "And you, General, first of all, because you are the only man who can give us practical assistance in our search for the *Italia*."

Nobile would remember those fatal words all his life. He

had not much cared for the idea of being the first man saved.
"Take Ceccioni first," he said. "He's injured too."
"No," said Lundborg. "But there's nothing to worry
about. Set your mind at rest. We'll come back and rescue
the others, one at a time. It won't take long now."
Nobile had imagined that a whole flight of planes would
set off to save his men, and, still unwillingly, he agreed to
be saved first. After all, it was perfectly true that he could be
of more assistance than anyone else in directing the search
for the missing *Italia* and the men on board her.
But it had turned out that only Lundborg's plane was of
any use for landing and taking off on ice. The other available
plane was too heavy and its pilot, the Finn, Sarko, declared
that it was quite impossible for him to touch down or take
off with it in such a confined space.
"What you need are those small British planes, the *Moths*,
fitted out with skis."
Nobile immediately despatched an urgent message for
Moths to be sent. But how long would it take before they
could be ready? Even with Lundborg's small plane, the
rescue would only have been a matter of time if things had
gone well. But they had not gone well, and now Lundborg
and his plane were helpless on the ice. At the same time the
Krassin had come to a standstill.
But what about its aeroplane, couldn't that make a search?
Nobile begged Samoilovitch to make the attempt and the
Russian agreed. On 8th July the first flight was made. On
10th July the plane set off again with the triple task of finding
the red tent, finding the Malmgren group and discovering
the whereabouts of the *Italia*.
Two hours after its departure the pilot Tchuknovski
radioed that the plane was returning. Up till that time nothing had been found and the dreaded Arctic mist had begun
to close in again.

In the meantime, work had been going forward to prepare the *Krassin* to move again and steam was already being got up in the boilers. Denser clouds of smoke rose from her two funnels and signal bonfires were set burning on the ice to guide Tchuknovski back to the ship. Instructions were sent out by wireless: *We are waiting for you. Reply.*

At first there was no reply and on board the *Krassin* they were beginning to fear that this terrible business had claimed further victims. Anxiously the wireless operator tuned in. Then suddenly he began to scribble. He wrote down three words only; it was all he had been able to catch. At first he read the three words without comprehension. Then he gave an exclamation and hurried off with his pad to Professor Samoilovitch. The three words were: *Group Malmgren . . . Charles . . .*

It was quite clear that Tchuknovski had spotted the Malmgren group in the neighbourhood of Charles XII Island. The men had been missing for five weeks and the world had given them up as lost. But they were alive after all. It was incredible news.

Back again at his apparatus, the wireless operator tried to make contact with Tchuknovski again: *Give us further details. Are they alive and well? And where are you? Don't leave us in uncertainty . . .*

It was a quarter to seven now, but Tchuknovski made no reply. Samoilovitch waited in the W/T cabin beside the operator, anxious to hear whatever news there was at once. Each passing minute reduced the chances of a safe return of Tchuknovski's plane. The wireless of the *Krassin* went on calling for five hours. It seemed quite clear now that Tchuknovski and his crew were lost with their plane.

"Carry on all the same," ordered Samoilovitch as he finally left the cabin. The operator went on trying, but without much hope. But it was a day of miracles. Shortly before midnight Tchuknovski spoke again: he had seen the Malmgren group from the air. Two men had made signals to him. Unfortunately he had been compelled to make a forced landing near Cape Wrede. He and his companions were safe. They could wait. The most urgent task was to pick up the Malmgren group.

Samoilovitch did not hesitate. Despite the damage the *Krassin* had suffered, despite the risks involved and despite the warnings of the captain, he ordered the ship to make with all possible speed for Charles XII Island where the Malmgren group was reported to be still alive. Once again the *Krassin* forged forward, met the shock of ice, broke through and withdrew for the next run. And so on and on. At last she came near Charles XII Island. All the men who were not kept elsewhere by their duties were on deck now, eagerly scanning the wastes of ice ahead and abreast of them and almost fighting for the privilege of mounting into the crow's nest, for Samoilovitch had promised a handsome bonus to the first man to spot the Malmgren group.

The siren of the *Krassin* was wailing hoarsely like some prehistoric monster, booming and echoing over the ice in a desperate attempt to break the vast silence and guide the marooned men to safety. Several times the watching sailors began to shout madly in the belief that they had spotted something, but always it turned out to be birds, a bear or just shadows—never the men staggering along to safety over the ice.

The vain wait, the repeatedly dashed hopes, the constant booming of the siren, strained everyone's nerves. On board the *Krassin* they began to wonder whether Tchuknovski had made a mistake, perhaps been deceived as they had been several times. After all, it was really too good to be true that they should save three men the world had long given up for lost. No one shouted now; the men were silent as they continued to stare. No one wanted to be disappointed again. Then came a shout. This time it was from the pilot, Breitkopf, a veteran of the Arctic seas, not a man to make mistakes.

The report created tremendous excitement on board and everyone stared in the direction in which Breitkopf was pointing. He was right: a figure could be seen distinctly through binoculars. A man dancing like a madman and waving his arms. In one hand he had a piece of stuff which he was using as a flag.

"No doubt about it this time," said Samoilovitch with satisfaction, and the *Krassin* changed course towards what was now seen to be two men. The second man had been lying stretched out on the ice, but he dragged himself to his feet with obvious difficulty and began to wave too, as though he feared he might be overlooked.

"There should be three of them," said Samoilovitch, who was studying the two men through his glasses. "There were Malmgren, Zappi and Mariano. I can't see a third. Could it be Sora and Van Dongen after all?"

When the *Krassin* was close enough a small party was landed. They came up with the two men on the ice.

"Are you Malmgren?" asked the Russian officer in charge, addressing the man they had first seen.

At first neither of them seemed to understand. They shook hands jerkily with their rescuers and spoke rapidly in a language the Russians did not understand. It was Italian. The Russians made out that the one man was Zappi and the other Mariano. The interrogation proceeded mostly in sign language. Where was Malmgren? Malmgren? Zappi pointed to the sea and jabbed down his thumb.

Malmgren had perished! The Russians subsequently discovered that he had died in such circumstances that at first they were afraid to probe too deeply for fear of finding out the full truth.

181

Whilst Mariano was hoisted on board the *Krassin*, Zappi, who had come on board without assistance, was talking volubly, thanking Samoilovitch, joking and asking for something to eat and drink. Under pressure he finally consented to tell them something of Malmgren's end.

"Ah, that was a man!" he exclaimed. "A real man. He gave me his compass as a souvenir."

"Yes, yes," agreed Samoilovitch a trifle impatiently, "but how did he come to die?"

"He died like a man."

"I've no doubt," said Samoilovitch drily, "but under what circumstances?"

"He was exhausted. He was unwilling to spoil our chances of survival and he ordered us to go on without him."

"And you did?"

"What else could we do? We had to obey. Our first duty was to make contact with the rescue parties in order that General Nobile and the others could be saved."

"So Malmgren was still alive when you left him?"

"He asked me to dig him a grave, put him in it and give him the *coup de grace* with a hatchet. He didn't want to suffer any longer."

Samoilovitch felt his blood run cold at this story.

"And did you obey him that time, too?" he persisted.

"No. We went away. When we turned round he made signs that we should go on."

That concluded Samoilovitch's inquiries for the time being. The two men were taken to the sick-bay where it was discovered that Zappi, the fit man, was wearing many garments, his own and those of Malmgren, whereas his comrade Mariano was insufficiently clothed and half-frozen, and that although Zappi declared that he had eaten nothing for thirteen days, it could have been no more than five or six at the most.

Ugly rumours began to circulate on board the *Krassin*, and when they reached Europe, people were deeply shocked. Why was Zappi lying? Why was he so anxious to mislead his rescuers about the length of his fast? Had he . . . ?

"I can scarcely believe it," said Samoilovitch in answer to the question they hardly dared formulate. "Malmgren died a fortnight ago, and at that time their food was not entirely exhausted."

But it was from Zappi that they had learned when Malmgren died. Supposing this was not true either? Supposing Malmgren had been dead only a week?

The *Krassin* was making the best possible speed now towards the ice-floe on which Lundborg and Nobile's abandoned companions were still waiting to be rescued. In the meantime Zappi talked loudly, repeating his account of the death of Malmgren and snubbing a Russian sailor who had happened to call him "comrade".

"He compelled us to leave him," he insisted. "We had to obey. Ah, that was a man!"

When Mariano was questioned after he had recovered a little he merely confirmed what Zappi said, but the Russians were not satisfied—there was something very much like fear in his eyes.

"Poor Mariano!" exclaimed Zappi. "He wanted me to leave him, too. He had already left me his things . . ."

Samoilovitch shrugged his shoulders and asked no more questions. After all, he was a scientist, not a policeman. Official investigators must try to discover the truth later. For the moment his duty was to do everything possible to save the other marooned men.

The *Krassin* continued to break her way through the ice, leaving behind her a long, black trail of water through the Arctic wastes. They were no longer going forward by guess now; they knew the approximate position of the famous red tent. Biagi's little short-wave apparatus was unable to reach the *Krassin* and so the base ship *Citta di Milano* was acting as wireless telephone intermediary: *Proceed along the same course. You are thirty miles from the tent . . . You are twenty miles from the tent . . . You are three miles from the tent . . .*

"In that case we ought to be able to see it," replied Samoilovitch, "but we can see nothing."

"They can see you already," came the reply. "They are a few miles to the south-west."

At 20.15 hours on 14th July the look-out of the *Krassin* spotted the survivors of the *Italia*: "black specks moving against a background of ice, as though on a cinema screen". Gradually the details of a scene that had held the attention of the world for the past two months became clearer: there was the red tent, the aerial of Biagi's wireless, the abandoned parachutes that had been used to drop supplies, Lundborg's little plane with its tail in the air and its nose embedded in the ice—Lundborg himself was no longer there, a comrade having taken him off a day or so earlier. All the details stood out against a stark décor of ice that might have been the scene of another tragedy. The actors were standing there with smiling faces turned towards the black mass of the icebreaker as it moved in to rescue them. Only one man of the group was not in the crowd waving to the rescuers, and that was the wireless operator Biagi. He was sitting at his apparatus sending out the message he had dreamed of so often, hardly daring to believe that one day he would send it out in reality. But the moment had come:

Italia here. Italia here. We are saved now. The Krassin has arrived. We are saved, saved, saved . . .

The situation gradually cleared up—except for the Malmgren affair. In all, seven men of the Nobile expedition were saved. Other good news also came in. The *Malygin* recovered her lost plane, with the crew safe and sound. Sora and Van Dongen were also found alive.

Then on 17th July it was reported that the *Krassin* had discovered the remains of the *Italia* with the other eight men of her crew. But this report turned out to be false. The period of miracles was over; the period of canards was beginning again.

"Go on with the search," Nobile urged Professor Samoilovitch. "My dirigible can't be far away."

But the Russian scientist knew more about Arctic conditions and polar drift than the Italian aeronaut: in the space of two months the polar drift could have carried the crashed *Italia* a very long way indeed.

However, he too was prepared to admit that it was not easy for a large airship to disappear without trace, even in the vast expanses of the Arctic. Nevertheless, he had to give up the search and return to his base to repair the damage the *Krassin* had suffered. "We shall be back," he promised.

Other search ships took over the quest. The French, who were very interested in the fate of their *Latham* and its crew, sent the *Strasbourg* and the *Quentin-Roosevelt*, followed on 4th July by the *Pourquoi-pas?*

"Things are far from hopeless," said their commander. "I am positive of that. I am sure that Guilbaud and his companions will return safe and sound. If the machine succeeded in making a normal landing, then with a man like Amundsen we have every right to be hopeful."

"If the machine succeeded in making a normal landing" — that condition alone was enough to discount the Frenchman's optimism. In the ice Amundsen would naturally know what to do, but supposing the *Latham* had crashed in the sea far away from land and far away from shipping lanes, what then? Even Amundsen's great resourcefulness and experience would be of little use.

ROBERT DE LA CROIX

People didn't care to think about it, and yet they did not
believe that the search would prove successful. "Only an
ice-breaker," Amundsen himself had said.

False reports continued to come in, to add to the confusion.
People were prepared to believe anything at first without
even considering its probability. One ship reported having
sighted the *Latham* drifting; the wireless-operator of another
thought he had received a message from Guilbaud. A group
of seal-hunters swore that they had seen signal rockets rising
over the ice in the distance. Others had seen signals in the
mist. And there were clairvoyants who declared that they
were in touch with Amundsen every evening after dark . . .

But amidst this welter of conflicting reports, veteran
explorers were preparing to launch a systematic search.
One after the other the old comrades of Amundsen from the
Gjöa, the *Maud*, the *Fram*, and the *Norge* made their way
towards Spitzbergen to join forces there.

"We couldn't let Roald down if there were only one
chance in a thousand," was typical of their views. They
prepared and equipped the whaler *Veslekari*, and as it
steamed north another party travelled south towards Italy—
Nobile and the survivors of his expedition were passing
through Europe on their way home. The Italian Government had strictly forbidden them to communicate with
anyone at all on the way. At the stations where the train
stopped, a silent crowd of spectators surrounded their
carriage. In Germany, on the day they passed through,
a newspaper published a cartoon depicting Nobile, Zappi
and Mariano with bared teeth behind bars and the inscription, *The cannibals*.

It was the death of Malmgren and its attendant circumstances that worried men's minds more than anything else.
The *Daily News* was expressing the general opinion when it
wrote,

The Death of Amundsen

The sombre North Pole drama the whole world has followed with such painful interest has certain elements of mystery. The best way to clear up the whole matter and restore the good name of the parties concerned would be to institute an impartial investigation as speedily as possible.

In Copenhagen the *Politiken* called for the setting up of an international tribunal composed of experienced polar explorers to examine Nobile's conduct of the expedition.

The Swedish Government made a diplomatic *démarche* requesting the Italian Government to provide an exact account of the fashion in which the Swedish citizen Malmgren met his death.

But the Italian Press indignantly rejected all demands for an investigation of the disagreeable incidents:

The account given by Zappi and Mariano of their tragic parting from their Swedish comrade in the epic march towards North East Land cannot and must not become the centre of any discussion whatsoever. Their word must be believed, as Nansen was believed; just as the word of all other explorers was believed when they were unable to provide any other witnesses to the truth of what they said beyond their own honour and reputation.

Zappi was very voluble in his own defence. He even went to visit Malmgren's mother.

"Your son and I were like brothers," he assured her. "I have been much mortified by all the things that have been said about me, but my conscience is clear before God. Your son was not in very good physical shape even when we started and it was not long before he began to realize that his strength was failing him. Then there came a day—I believe it was 12th June—when he asked me to do him one final service: to dig him a grave in the snow, and he gave me his compass, a memento of his voyage with Amundsen on board the *Maud*."

And Zappi added: "You knew him—we had no alternative but to obey him. He was that sort of man. A real man."

He subsequently claimed that Malmgren's mother had believed him, but whether this was so or not, public opinion was far from convinced, and attacks in the Press continued against Nobile, against Zappi and against the whole expedition. The Italian newspaper *Impero* belligerently proposed a duel between ten Italian journalists and ten foreign journalists to avenge the honour of Italy.

Even the Italian Fascist Government found this suggestion a trifle too ridiculous, and under its disapproval nothing more was heard of a proposal that would probably have developed into a farce. In reply to world demands for an investigation, it announced that an inquiry would be held. "But," it added, "the Commission of Inquiry will be composed of Italians only. We are not prepared to tolerate the interference of any other nation."

The reply to this was obvious, and the world Press pointed out that the men who had lost their lives had by no means all been Italians; Swedish, Norwegian and French lives had been lost too. The world had a right to know the truth—the whole truth.

The Italians now began to quarrel among themselves. Nobile charged Romagna, the captain of his base ship, *Citta di Milano*, with negligence, and in fact it was discovered that only two days after the disaster one of the wireless operators of the *Citta di Milano* had actually received a truncated message from Biagi, the wireless operator of the *Italia*, and that it had been ignored because it was complacently assumed to have been sent out by a wireless station in Libya.

Whilst this distressing and deplorable squabble was going on, the searchers in the far north were continuing their work. The *Veslekari* systematically explored all the islands around Spitzbergen, quartering the ice over vast areas and leaving no likely spot unsearched. As soon as she was ready, the

The Death of Amundsen

Krassin put to sea again. The drama of the *Italia* was played out now, and all attention was concentrated on the great shade of Amundsen. But this time there were to be no miracles, no unexpected discoveries. The searchers found nothing whatever, though there was the usual plethora of hallucinations and legends that grow up around all mysterious disappearances. As far as his anxiously searching friends were concerned, Amundsen had vanished from the face of the earth without trace.

And then on 1st September the mate of a fishing smack spotted something round and black rolling over and over in the swell.

"It's probably only an oil barrel," said the skipper when his attention was drawn to it. "Not worth wasting time on."

"I don't know," objected the mate. "It's got a funny shape for an oil barrel. Much too long I should say. Better have a look at it."

And they did.

"We shall never forget the moment when we pulled it in and saw what it was," said the skipper afterwards. "It wasn't an oil barrel as I had at first thought, but the float of a hydroplane."

As soon as the skipper realized what it was, he turned about and hurried back to Tromsö, where he arrived in the early hours of the morning. The Norwegian authorities took charge of the float, and it was examined by experts. It was certainly the float of a hydroplane and probably that of the lost *Latham*, but the experts could not be sure.

The engineer who had overhauled the *Latham* during its stop at Bergen was consulted.

"We had to put a small copper patch on one of the floats," he said. "It leaked. If that happened to be the one . . ."

The small copper patch was discovered. It happened to be the one.

The experts then began to construct their theories. The float was intact and undamaged, and from this they argued that if the *Latham* had crashed and sunk then the float would have been crushed in by the pressure of the water at depth. But if the *Latham* had touched down successfully then the float, which was firmly attached to the undercarriage, would not have come loose on its own. It had, therefore, probably been deliberately detached to serve as a raft—or perhaps to carry a message.

A message? No one had thought of that, so when the only relic of Guilbaud and his companions arrived in Paris, the French authorities had it carefully opened. It contained nothing.

Hopes were dashed again. This was probably the end. What could be expected now—further finds?

On 18th October another fishing-boat fished a spare petrol-tank out of the water. This time no expert examination was necessary to discover its origin. A plain inscription was painted on it: *Petrol capacity 600 litres. Hydroplane Latham.* Something else was written on it in chalk, but the words were much defaced. All that could be deciphered was: *Accie . . . 20. XI . . .* Was that the date of the accident perhaps?

Inquiries immediately instituted showed the chalk markings to ante-date the disappearance. They had no reference to what had happened.

The search went on in Arctic waters, but at last, unwilling hands had to swing the wheel and put the *Veslekari* on her homeward course. This was really the end. It was quite true that where polar disappearances were concerned, hope need not be abandoned for a very long time—a space of years even. But in this case it was probably a question of a common mishap to an aeroplane. That was very different. In any case, the year was advancing now and the cold was whitening the sea as the ice extended its domain.

The Death of Amundsen

During the winter, hope rose again without any particular reason. People imagined a few men huddled together under a small tent and a little distance away from them, a second group of men encamped beside the wreckage of an airship. The last actors in the latest drama of the frozen north. Perhaps in the spring they would return.

The spring of the following year produced nothing of any importance—unless the report of the official Italian commission of inquiry can be regarded as contributing anything to the affair. It informed a sceptical world that the conduct of Zappi and Mariano had been "entirely praiseworthy", but it publicly dropped General Nobile, who was made responsible for the loss of his airship.

Nobile protested indignantly against the verdict of the commission and resigned his rank. Shortly afterwards, he left Italy to work in Soviet Russia, still protesting, and bitterly reproaching his compatriots for their injustice and ingratitude.

With the better weather, polar explorers again pushed north beyond Spitzbergen, but for all their searching they discovered nothing—though this did not prevent the circulation of the usual story of the mysterious white man living amongst the Eskimos as one of their own. Who could he be, if not Amundsen?

Veteran Norwegian seamen and explorers shrugged their shoulders at the ridiculous tale. Amundsen had been a kind of Viking god for Norway, and gods don't bury themselves; a Viking hero would leave for Valhalla one evening when mist shrouded the sea, and after that no more would ever be heard of him.

A Dissertation on the Art of Flying

DR SAMUEL JOHNSON

In his wanderings in the Happy Valley in search of tranquillity and en-lightenment, Prince Rasselas of Abyssinia came across a craftsman with a novel idea for a flying apparatus. Although Dr Johnson, with characteristic irony, causes the inventor to crash ignominiously—and wet his wings if not singe them—it is interesting that even in the eigh-teenth century, when he was writing, long before flying became a reality, men should fear that mastery of the air might be put to malign uses.

Among the artists that had been allured into the Happy Valley, to labour for the accommodation and pleasure of its inhabitants, was a man eminent for his knowledge of the mechanic powers, who had contrived many engines both of use and recreation. By a wheel which the stream turned, he forced the water into a tower, whence it was distributed to all the apartments of the palace. He erected a pavilion in the garden, around which he kept the air always cool by artificial showers. One of the groves, appropriated to the ladies, was ventilated by fans, to which the rivulets that ran through it gave a constant motion; and instruments of soft music were played at proper distances, of which some played by the impulse of the wind, and some by the power of the stream.

This artist was sometimes visited by Rasselas, who was pleased with every kind of knowledge, imagining that the time would come when all his acquisitions should be of use to him in the open world. He came one day to amuse himself in his usual manner, and found the master busy in building a sailing chariot. He saw that the design was practicable upon a level surface, and with expressions of great esteem solicited its completion.

The workman was pleased to find himself so much regarded by the Prince, and resolved to gain yet higher honours.

"Sir," said he, "you have seen but a small part of what the mechanic sciences can perform. I have been long of the opinion that, instead of the tardy conveyance of ships and chariots, man might use the swifter migration of wings; that the fields of air are open to knowledge, and that only ignorance and idleness need crawl upon the ground."

This hint rekindled the Prince's desire of passing the mountains. Having seen what the mechanist had already performed, he was willing to fancy that he could do more; yet resolved to inquire further before he suffered hope to afflict him by disappointment.

"I am afraid", said he to the artist, "that your imagination prevails over your skill, and that you now tell me rather what you wish than what you know. Every animal has his element assigned him; the birds have the air, and man and beasts the earth."

"So", replied the mechanist, "fishes have the water, in which yet beasts can swim by nature and man by art. He that can swim needs not despair to fly; to swim is to fly in a grosser fluid, and to fly is to swim in a subtler. We are only to proportion our power of resistance to the different density of matter through which we are to pass. You will be necessarily upborne by the air if you can renew any impulse upon it faster than the air can recede from the pressure."

"But the exercise of swimming", said the Prince, "is very laborious; the strongest limbs are soon wearied. I am afraid the act of flying will be yet more violent; and wings will be of no great use unless we can fly further than we can swim."

"The labour of rising from the ground", said the artist, "will be great, as we see it in the heavier domestic fowls; but as we mount higher, the Earth's attraction and the body's gravity will be gradually diminished, till we shall arrive at a region where the man shall float in the air without any tendency to fall; no care will then be necessary but to move forward, which the gentlest impulse will effect. You, sir, whose curiosity is so extensive, will easily conceive with what pleasure a philosopher, furnished with wings and hovering in the sky, would see the Earth and all its inhabitants rolling beneath him, and presenting to him successively, by its diurnal motion, all the countries within the same parallel. How must it amuse the pendent spectator to see the moving scene of land and ocean, cities and deserts; to survey with equal security the marts of trade and the fields of battle; mountains infested by barbarians, and fruitful regions gladdened by plenty and lulled by peace. How easily shall we then trace the Nile through all his passages, pass over to distant regions, and examine the face of Nature from one extremity of the earth to the other."

"All this", said the Prince, "is much to be desired, but I am afraid that no man will be able to breathe in these regions of speculation and tranquillity. I have been told that respiration is difficult upon lofty mountains; yet from these precipices, though so high as to produce great tenuity of air, it is very easy to fall; therefore I suspect that from any height where life can be supported, there may be danger of too quick descent."

"Nothing", replied the artist, "will ever be attempted if all possible objections must be first overcome. If you will favour my project, I will try the first flight at my own hazard. I have considered the structure of all volant animals, and find the folding continuity of the bat's wings most easily accommodated to the human form. Upon this model I shall begin my task tomorrow; and in a year expect to tower into the air beyond the malice and pursuit of man. But I will work only on this condition: that you shall not require me to make wings for any but ourselves."

"Why", said Rasselas, "should you envy others so great an advantage? All skill ought to be exerted for universal good; every man has owed much to others, and ought to repay the kindness that he has received."

"If men were all virtuous," returned the artist, "I should with great alacrity teach them to fly. But what would be the security of the good if the bad could at pleasure invade them from the sky? Against an army sailing through the clouds, neither walls, mountains, nor seas could afford security. A flight of northern savages might hover in the wind, and light with irresistible violence upon the capital of a fruitful region. Even this valley, the retreat of princes, the abode of happiness, might be violated by the sudden descent of some of the naked nations that swarm on the coast of the southern sea!"

The Prince promised secrecy, and waited for the performance, not wholly hopeless of success.

He visited the work from time to time, observed its progress, and remarked many ingenious contrivances to facilitate motion, and unite levity with strength. The artist was every day more certain that he should leave vultures and eagles behind him, and the contagion of his confidence seized upon the Prince. In a year the wings were finished; and on a morning appointed the maker appeared, furnished for flight, on a little promontory: he waved his pinions a while to gather air, then leaped from his stand, and in an instant dropped into the lake. His wings, which were of no use in the air, sustained him in the water; and the Prince drew him to land half-dead with terror and vexation.

Terror Falls from the Skies

CONSTANTINE FITZGIBBON

Here in this extract about the London blitz is justification of Prince Rasselas's fears that a successful flying-machine might be the means of spreading terror from the air. The parachuted land-mine described here was one of the most terrifying weapons used in conventional bombing, but of course the atomic bombs dropped on Hiroshima and Nagasaki made that seem old-fashioned, while the hideous defoliation policy carried out in Vietnam added a new horror the Prince would have found unimaginable.

The German attack on London would have been much more cruel in 1940, had they not had to rely chiefly on comparatively light bombs. They were well aware of this, and one expedient that they used was to drop sea-mines by parachute against land targets.

The magnetic mine had been Hitler's first "secret weapon" of the war, and had caused very heavy losses of shipping during the winter of 1939–40. It had been largely mastered, through the degaussing of ships and other means, by the summer of 1940, though it was still a menace. The original method of delivery had been for surface vessels to sow their mines in British coastal waters, but in November of 1939 seaplanes began to drop them by parachute. Later land-planes were also used for this purpose, the *Heinkel 111*s of *Kampfgeschwader 4* being equipped each to carry two magnetic mines, slung beneath their wings on either side of the fuselage. By the time the Blitz began these magnetic mines, as weapons in the sea war, were becoming obsolescent, and since the Germans lacked a big blast bomb, they immediately began to use them against land targets. On the very first day of the Blitz, *KG4* and other bomber groups were dropping mines on parachutes into the dock area; according to a pilot of that group, he and his comrades were thenceforth usually taken off their normal mine-laying duties whenever there was a major raid on London and were sent out as an ordinary bomber group, sometimes with bombs, sometimes with mines. In the beginning these mines were dropped complete with sea-fuses, though later the sea-fuses were removed. This expenditure of mines against land targets did not altogether please the German Navy.

On 20th September Admiral Raeder told Hitler, "At present numerous aerial mines are being dropped on London. They have a decided effect, to be sure; however, the time has come for large-scale mine operations, since the new type of fuse is now available in sufficient quantities." This is a reference to the acoustic fuse. The *Luftwaffe*, wishing to use the mines as bombs, pulled the other way, and by 14th October Hitler had ordered a compromise whereby the Air Force was allowed to drop the "old sort of mine" over London on moonlit nights, when, presumably, these expensive objects could, in theory at least, be aimed at targets of commensurate value. And throughout the Blitz these great cylinders, weighing a ton or a ton and a half each, came silently swinging down on their parachutes through the night skies on to the streets and houses of the capital.

It is a curious coincidence that whereas Hitler ordered that they be dropped on moonlit nights in order that some accuracy be obtained, Churchill, four weeks earlier, on

19th September, had written in a memorandum for the Chiefs of Staff Committee,

The dropping of large mines by parachute proclaims the enemy's entire abandonment of all pretence of aiming at military objectives. At 5,000 feet he cannot have the slightest idea what he is going to hit. This, therefore, proves the "act of terror" intention against the civil population.

Certainly these mines, called almost universally and quite incorrectly "land-mines", did inspire great terror. This was due primarily to the violence of the explosion, no part of which was muffled (as with the occasional bombs of similar weight then being dropped) by burial in the ground; but a secondary cause was the usual spooky silence with which those lethal monsters came floating down. For instance one that dropped, silently, on to Park Hill recreation grounds in Croydon, on 28th September, broke all the windows in the High Street, a good ten minutes' walk away.

And here is a description of another, which fell outside the BBC in Langham Place, and destroyed, among other buildings, the old Langham Hotel. It is a transcript of a recording made for the BBC during the war. The narrator is a man, and few people who were so close to a mine when it exploded can have survived to tell the tale:

"On the night of 8th December 1940, I left the BBC shortly after ten forty-five and accompanied by a colleague went to the cycle-shed in Chapel Mews. The customary nightly air-raid was in progress, and as we left the cycle-shed we could hear the distant sound of aircraft and A.A. gunfire. We were just entering Hallam Street from the mews when I heard the shrieking, whistling noise like a large bomb falling. This noise continued for about three seconds, and then abruptly ceased as if in mid-air. There was no thud, explosion or vibration. I particularly remember this, as I'd heard this happen once before, and was curious as to what caused it and why it stopped. Then came the sound of something clattering down the roof of a building in the direction of Broadcasting House. I looked up, thinking that it might be incendiaries, but this was not so. We slowly walked round to the entrance of Broadcasting House, and I estimate that we took about three and a half minutes in doing so. My colleague went inside, returned the cycle-shed keys, and cycled off towards Oxford Street. I remained outside the entrance, talking to two policemen, and enquiring about possible diversions on my route home. Their names were Vaughan and Clarke. A saloon car was parked alongside the kerb, some distance round from the entrance, and I could see to the left of the car the lamp-post in the middle of the road opposite the Langham Hotel. The policemen had their backs to this, so did not observe what followed. Whilst we were conversing I noticed a large, dark, shiny object approach the lamp-post and then recede. I concluded that it was a taxi parking. It made no noise. The night was clear, with a few small clouds. There was moonlight from a westerly direction, but Portland Place was mainly shadow. All three of us were wearing our steel helmets; my chin-strap was round the back of my head, as I had been advised to wear it so, shortly after I was issued with the helmet.

"A few seconds later I saw what seemed to be a very large tarpaulin of a drab khaki colour fall on the same spot; the highest part of it was about ten or twelve feet above the road when I first saw it, and it seemed to be about twenty-five feet across. It fell at about the speed of a pocket handkerchief when dropped, and made no noise. Repair work was being carried out on Broadcasting House and I concluded that it was a tarpaulin which had become detached and had fallen from the building into the roadway. There were no other warnings of any imminent danger. I drew the attention of the policemen to it. They turned round and could see nothing. It had collapsed and from where we were it was partly screened by the car, and the roadway at that point was in shadow. They told me that they could not see anything. Then followed some banter, but I persisted in saying that I had seen something fall in the road. They then decided to go to investigate. A third policeman, Mortimer, had meanwhile approached us—he was about to conduct a lady across that part of the road. But after hearing that I'd seen something, he told me he was taking her inside the building while they found out what it was. Vaughan drew ahead of Clarke, who stopped at the kerb to ask me just exactly where it had dropped. I went over towards him, calling out that I would show him it. It was about a minute since I'd seen the dark object. I went towards the tarpaulin, as I thought it was, and had reached the spot to the left of Clarke about six feet from the kerb, and twenty-five to thirty feet from 'the thing', when Vaughan came running towards me at high speed. He shouted something which I did not hear. At that moment there was a loud, swishing noise, as if a plane were diving with engine cut off—or like a gigantic fuse burning. It lasted about three or four seconds; it did not come from the lamp-post end of 'the thing' but it may have come from the other end.

"Vaughan passed me on my left and Clarke, who apparently had understood the shout, also ran towards the building. Realizing that I would have to turn right about before I could start running, I crouched down in what is known as 'prone-falling position number one'. Even at that moment I did not imagine that there was any danger in the road, and thought that it was coming from above, up Portland Place. My head was up watching, and before I could reach position number two and lie down flat, the thing in the road exploded. I had a momentary glimpse of a large ball of blinding, wild, white light and two concentric rings of colour, the inner one lavender and the outer one violet, as I ducked my head. The ball seemed to be ten to twenty feet high, and was near the lamp-post. Several things happened simultaneously. My head was jerked back due to a heavy blow on the dome and rim of the back of my steel helmet, but I do not remember this, for, as my head went back, I received a severe blow on my forehead and the bridge of my nose. The blast bent up the front rim of my helmet and knocked it off my head. The explosion made an indescribable noise—something like a colossal growl—and was accompanied by a veritable tornado of air blast. I felt an excruciating pain in my ears, and all sounds were replaced by a very loud, singing noise, which I was told later was when I lost my hearing and had my eardrums perforated. I felt that consciousness was slipping from me, and that moment I heard a clear, loud voice shouting, 'Don't let yourself go, face up to it—hold on.' It rallied me, and summoning all my willpower and energy I succeeded in forcing myself down into a crouching position with my knees on the ground and my feet against the kerb behind me and my hands covering my face.

"I remember having to move them over my ears because of the pain in them, doubtless due to the blast. This seemed to ease the pain. Then I received another hit on the forehead and felt weaker. The blast seemed to come in successive waves, accompanied by vibrations from the ground. I felt as if it were trying to spin me and clear me away from the kerb. Then I received a very heavy blow just in front of the right temple which knocked me down flat on my side, in the gutter. Later, in our first-aid post, they removed what they described as a piece of bomb from that wound. Whilst in the gutter I clung on to the kerb with both hands and with my feet against it. I was again hit in the right chest, and later found that my double-breasted overcoat, my coat, leather comb-case and papers had been cut through, and the watch in the top right-hand pocket of my waistcoat had the back dented in and its works broken.

"Just as I felt that I could not hold out much longer, I realized that the blast pressure was decreasing and a shower of dust, dirt and rubble swept past me. Pieces penetrated my face, some skin was blown off, and something pierced my left thumbnail and my knuckles were cut, causing me involuntarily to let go my hold on the kerb. Instantly, although the blast was dying down, I felt myself being slowly blown across the pavement towards the wall of the building. I tried to hold on but there was nothing to hold on to. Twice I tried to rise but seemed held down. Eventually I staggered to my feet. I looked around and it seemed like a scene from Dante's *Inferno*. The front of the building was lit by a reddish-yellow light; the saloon car was on fire to the left of me, and the flames from it were stretching out towards the building, and not upwards; pieces of brick, masonry and glass seemed to appear on the pavement, making—to me—no sound; a few dark, huddled bodies were round about, and right in front of me were two soldiers; one, some feet from a breach in the wall of the building where a fire seemed to be raging, was propped up against the wall with his arms dangling, like a rag doll.

"The other was nearer, about twelve feet from the burning car; he was sitting up with his knees drawn up and supporting himself by his arms—his trousers had been blown off him. I could see that his legs were bare and that he was wearing short grey underpants. He was alive and conscious.

"I told him to hang on to an upright at the entrance and to shout like hell for assistance, should he see or hear anyone approaching. I went back to look at the other soldier. He was still in the same posture and I fear that he was dead. I looked around. There was a long, dark body lying prone, face downward, close to the kerb in front of the building—it may have been Vaughan. There appeared to be one or two dark, huddled bodies by the wall of the building. I had not the strength to lift any of them. I wondered where the water was coming from which I felt dripping down my face, and soon discovered that it was blood from my head wounds. I could see no movement anywhere, and thought I would look round for my steel helmet and gas mask, which I had slung round me at the time of the explosion. I soon found the gas mask and picked up a steel helmet which I later found was not my own.

"I was then joined by my colleague who had returned, and went with him to the entrance where I shouted for assistance for those outside, and for someone to bring fire-fighting appliances to put out the car fire, as I was afraid the glare would bring down more bombs.

"I walked down to our First Aid Post, where I was treated, and then to Listening Hall I where I rested until I was taken away by the stretcher party and sent to the Middlesex Hospital. Here I received every possible attention and kindness. Later on I was told that 'the thing' had been a land-mine, and that its explosion or blast had lasted for *nine seconds*.

"The effect of the blast on my clothes is possibly of interest: I was wearing bicycle clips round the bottoms of my trousers at the time; after the blast was over, my double-breasted overcoat was slit up the back and torn in several places, but was being held together by the belt. My trousers and underpants were pitted with small cuts about an inch long, but presumably the bicycle clips had prevented the draught getting up my trousers and tearing them off. A woollen scarf, which was knotted round my neck, undoubtedly saved my neck and chest from small fragments, such as were removed from my face which was not covered . . ."

A little earlier on the same evening, a bomb had actually hit the BBC while Bruce Belfrage was reading the *nine o'clock news*. Though the crash was audible all round the world, the broadcasting equipment continued to function and Belfrage, with admirable sang-froid, to read the news. After the crash and a very brief pause, his voice was heard, impassive as ever: "The story of recent naval successes in the Mediterranean is told in an Admiralty communiqué issued tonight . . ."

The Airstrip at Konora

JAMES A. MICHENER

Kennedy—Heathrow—Orly—international airports are, it could almost be said, townships in their own right, with their gigantic and complex organizations for directing hundreds of immense aircraft and coping with millions of passengers every year. Konora, however, was an "airport" with a difference and though it might lack a V.I.P. lounge, its construction was typical of the enormous power and skill the United States was able to deploy in its war against the Japanese.

When Admiral Kester finally finished studying *Alligator* operations he said to himself, "They'll be wanting a bomber-strip at Konora to do the dirty work." He looked at his maps. Konora was a pin-point of an island, 320 miles from Kuralei. When you went into Konora, you tipped your hand. Japs would know you were headed somewhere important. But they wouldn't know whether your next step would be Kuralei, Truk, or Kavieng. Therefore, you would have some slight advantage.

But you'd have to move fast! From the first moment you set foot on Konora, you knew the weight of the entire Jap empire would rush to protect the next islands. You couldn't give the enemy much time. When you went into Konora, the chips were down. You batted out an airstrip in record time, or else . . .

At this point in his reasoning Admiral Kester asked me to get Commander Hoag, of the 144 SeaBees. Immediately. Soon Commander Hoag appeared. He was a big man, about six feet three, weighed well over 200 pounds, had broad shoulders, long legs, big hands, and bushy eyebrows. He wore his shirt with the top two buttons unfastened, so that he looked sloppy. But a mat of hair, showing on his chest, made you forget that. He was a Georgian man. Had been a contractor in Connecticut before the war. As a small boat enthusiast, he knew many Navy men. One of them had prevailed upon him to enter the SeaBees. To do so cost him $22,000 a year, for he was a wealthy man in civilian life. Yet he loved the order and discipline of Navy ways. He was forty-seven and had two children.

"Commander Hoag to see you, sir!" I reported.

"So soon?" the Admiral asked. "Bring him in."

Hoag loomed into the doorway and stepped briskly to the Admiral's desk. "You wished to see me, sir?" I started to go.

"Don't leave," Kester said. "I'll want you to serve as liaison on this job." The Admiral made no motion whereby we might be seated, so like schoolboys we stood before his rough desk.

"Hoag," he said briefly. "Can you build a bomber-strip on Konora?"

"Yessir!" Hoag replied, his eyes betraying his excitement.

"How do you know?" Kester inquired.

"I've studied every island in this area that could possibly have a bomber-strip. Konora would handle one. There are some tough problems, though. We'd have to round up all the Australians and missionaries who'd ever been there. Some tough questions about that island. Maps don't show much."

"Could the strip be completed for action within fifteen days of the minute you get your first trucks ashore?"

Without a moment's hesitation Hoag replied, "Yessir."

"Lay all preparations to do the job, Hoag. D-day will be in five weeks. You'll be the second echelon. You'll probably not need combat units, since the Marines should reduce the island in two days. But you'd better be prepared. Logistics and Intelligence will give you all the assistance you demand. You can write your own ticket, Hoag. But remember. Tremendous importance accrues to the time-table in this operation. Bombers must be ready to land on the sixteenth day."

"They will be," Hoag replied in a grim voice that came deep from his chest. "You can schedule them now."

"Very well!" the Admiral said. "I will."

I worked with Commander Hoag for the next five weeks. I was his errand boy, and scurried around to steal shipping space, essential tools, and key men. It was decided to throw the 144th and five maintenance units of SeaBees onto Konora. Some would build roads; others would knock down the jungle; others would haul coral; some would run electrical plants; important units would do nothing but keep gigantic machinery in operation; one batch of men would build living quarters.

"Coral worries me," Hoag said many times as he studied his maps. "I can't find records anywhere of coral pits on that island. Yet there must be. Damn it all, it would be the only island in that general region that didn't have some. Of course. Somewhere in our push north we're going to hit the island without coral. Then hell pips. But I just can't believe this island is it. One of those hills has got to have some coral. God!" he sighed. "It would be awful if we had to dig it all from sea-water. Get those experts in here again!"

When the experts on coral returned, Hoag was standing before a large map of Konora. The island was like a man's leg bent slightly at the knee. It looked something like a boomerang, but the joining knee was not so pronounced.

Neither leg was long enough for a bomber strip, which had to be at least 6,000 feet long. But by throwing the strip directly across the bend, the operation was possible. In this way it would cut across both legs. Since the enclosed angle pointed south, the strip would thus face due east and west. That was good for the winds in the region.

"Now, men," Hoag said wearily, "let's go over this damned thing again. The only place we can possibly build this strip is across the angle. The two legs are out. We all agree on that?" The men assented.

"That gives us two problems. First might be called the problem of the ravine. Lieut. Pearlstein, have you clarified your reasoning on that?"

Pearlstein, a very big Jewish boy, whom his men loved because of his willingness to raise hell on their behalf, moved to the map. His father had been a builder in New York. "Commander," he said, "I'm morally certain there must be a big ravine running north and south through that elbow. I'm sure of it, but the photographs don't show it. We can't find anyone who has been there. They always landed on the ends of the island. But look at the watershed! It's got to be that way!"

"I don't think so," a young ensign retorted. It was De Vito, from Columbus, Ohio. He graduated from Michigan and had worked in Detroit. There was a poll of the men. The general opinion was that there was no severe ravine on Konora.

"But, Commander," Pearlstein argued, "why not run the strip as far to the north as possible? Cut the length to 5,000 feet. If you keep it where you have it now, you'll get the extra length, that's right. But you're going to hit a ravine, I'm certain you will."

Commander Hoag spoke to me. "See if a strip 5,000 feet long would be acceptable," he ordered. I made proper inquiries among the air experts and was told that if no longer strip was humanly possible, 5,000 would have to do. But an extra thousand feet would save the lives of at least fifteen pilots. I reported this fact.

Everyone looked at Pearlstein. He countered with another proposal. "Then why not drop one end of the strip as far as possible down this east leg? You could still run the other end across the elbow. And you'd be so far north on the elbow that you'd miss the ravine."

"See if they could use a strip like that," I was told. "Let's see. Wind on take-off and landing would come from about 325 degrees."

I soon returned with information that our airmen considered 325 crosswind much less acceptable than earlier plans they had approved. "It's all right for an empty, normal plane," I reported. "But these bombers are going to be loaded to the last stretching ounce."

Hoag stood up. "Plans go ahead as organized. Now, as to the coral?" The commander and his officers gathered about the map. With red chalk he marked two hills, one at the northern tip of the elbow and one about half-way up the western leg. He then made many marks along the shoreline that lay within the bend of the knee.

"We can be pretty certain there will be coral here," he reasoned, indicating the shoreline. "But what do you think about these two hills?" His men argued the pros and cons of the hills. In some South Pacific islands SeaBees' work was made relatively easy by the discovery of some small mountains of solid coral. Then all they had to do was bull-doze the wonderful sea-rock loose, pile it on to trucks, haul it to where it was needed, and smash it flat with a roller. The result was a road, or a path, or a deck, or an airstrip, that almost matched cement. But on other islands, like Guadalcanal and Bourgainville for example, there was no coral, either in mountains or along the bays. Then the SeaBees swore and sweated, and for as long as Americans lived on those islands, they would eat lava dust, have it in their beds at night, and watch it disappear from their roads with every rain. If, as some Navy men had suggested, the country ought to build a monument to the SeaBees, the SeaBees should, in turn, build a monument to coral. It was their staunchest ally.

"The Australians are here, sir," a messenger announced.

Two long, thin men and one woman, old and un-pretty, stepped into the room. Commander Hoag gave the tired woman his chair. The men remained standing. They introduced themselves as Mr and Mrs Wilkins and Mr Heskwith. Eighteen years ago they had lived on Konora for three months. They were the only people we could find who knew the island.

It was quiet in the hot room as these three outposts of empire endeavoured to recall the scene of one of their many defeats in the islands. They had made no money there. The mosquitoes were unbearable. Trading boats refused to put into the lagoon. The natives were unfriendly. Mr Heskwith lost his wife on Konora. He had never remarried. Even though we were rushed, no one interrupted the dismal narrative.

The Wilkinses and Mr Heskwith had then gone to Guadalcanal. We wondered what had been the subtle arrangements between Mr Heskwith and Mrs Wilkins. Faded, in an ill-fitting dress, she seemed scarcely the magnet that would hold two men to her thatched hut for eighteen years. "At Guadalcanal we were doing nicely," Mr Wilkins concluded, "when the Japanese came. We saw them burn our place to the ground. We were up in the hills. My wife and I were some of the first to greet the American troops. Mr Heskwith, you see, was scouting with the native boys. He met your men later.

Mr Heskwith has been recommended for a medal of some kind by your naval forces. He was of great service to your cause."

Gaunt Mr Heskwith smiled in a sickly manner. We wondered what he could have done to help the United States Navy.

"Very well," Commander Hoag said. "We are proud to have you people and Mr Heskwith here to help us again. You understand that you will be virtual prisoners for the next four or five weeks. We are going to invade Konora shortly and are going to build a bomber-strip across the bend. Just as you see it on this map. We dare not risk any idle conversation about it. You'll be under guard till we land."

"Of course," Mr Wilkins said. "We were the other time, too."

The three Australians then studied the map in silence. We were abashed when Mrs Wilkins dryly observed, "I didn't know the island looked like that." We looked at one another.

"Now, point out where you lived," Commander Hoag suggested.

"It was here," Mr Wilkins said, making an X on the map.

"No," his wife corrected. "I'm sorry, David, but it was over here." They could not even agree as to which leg of the island they had settled on.

"Could you take the map down from the wall?" Mr Wilkins asked. "It might be easier to recall." Commander Hoag and one of his officers untacked the large map and placed it on the floor. "That's better!" Mr Wilkins said brightly. He and his wife walked around the map squinted at it, held their heads on one side. They could not agree. Mr Wilkins even found it difficult to believe that north was north.

"See!" Commander Hoag said quietly. "It's the same on other maps. That's north!" Still the Wilkinses could not determine where they had lived. "But try to think!" Hoag suggested. "Which way did the sun rise?"

"They asked us that in the other room, sir," Mrs Wilkins explained. "But we can't remember. It's been so long ago. And we wouldn't want to tell you anything that wasn't true."

"Mr Heskwith!" Hoag said suddenly. "Perhaps you could tell us something." The thin fellow was studying the western leg of the island. "Do you recall something now?" Hoag asked.

"I'm trying to find where it was we buried Marie," the man replied. "It was not far from a bay."

Hoag stepped aside as the three middle-aged people tried to recall even the slightest certainty about that far and unhappy chapter of their lives. No agreement was reached. No agreement could be reached. Time had dimmed the events. It was all right for people to say, "I can see it as plain as if it was yesterday." But some things, fortunately, do not remain as clear as they were yesterday. The mind obliterates them, as Konora had been obliterated.

"May I ask a question, sir?" Lieut. Pearlstein suggested. When the commander assented, he took the three Australians to the head of the map. "Now it would be very helpful if you could tell us something definite about this bend here. You see, the airstrip has to pass right over it. Were any of you ever in that region?"

All three volunteered to speak, but by consent granted eighteen years before, Mr Wilkins acted as chairman. "Yes," he said. "That's the logical place to settle. We went there first, didn't we? But we didn't like it."

"But why didn't you?" Pearlstein asked triumphantly.

"No breeze," Wilkins said briefly. Pearlstein's smile vanished.

"Did you ever go inland at this point?" he continued.

"Come to the question, Pearlstein," Hoag interrupted

impatiently. "What we need to know", he said in a kindly manner, "is whether or not there is a deep ravine across the bend?"

The Australians looked at one another blankly. Mutually, they began to shake their heads. "We wouldn't know that, sir," Mr Wilkins said.

"The only person likely to know that", Mrs Wilkins added, "is Mr Davenport."

"Who's Davenport?" Hoag demanded with some excitement.

"He's the New Zealander who lived on the island for about a dozen years," Mrs Wilkins explained.

"Why didn't we get Davenport up here?" Hoag demanded.

"Oh!" Mrs Wilkins explained. "The Japs caught him. And all his family."

Hoag was stumped. He spoke with Pearlstein a few minutes while the Australians studied the large map of the tiny island. Pearlstein returned to the map. "Can you think of anyone who might know about that bend?" he asked. "You can see how urgent it is that we satisfy our minds as to that ravine." The Australians wrinkled their brows.

"No," Mr Wilkins said aloud. "The skipper of the *Alceste* wouldn't be likely to know that."

"Not likely," Mrs Wilkins agreed.

It was Mr Heskwith who had the bright idea! He stepped forward hesitatingly. "Why don't you send one of us back to the island?" he suggested.

"Yes!" the Wilkinses agreed. They all stepped a few paces forward, towards Commander Hoag. He was taken aback by the proposal.

"There are Japs on the island. Hundreds of them," he said roughly.

"We know!" Mrs Wilkins replied.

"You think you could make it?" Pearlstein asked.

"We could try," Mr Wilkins said. It was as if he had volunteered to go to the corner for groceries.

"You have submarines to do things like that, don't you?" Mrs Wilkins asked.

"Do you mean that you three would go up there?" Commander Hoag asked, incredulously.

"Yes," Mr Wilkins replied, establishing himself as the authority.

"I think I should go," Mr Heskwith reasoned.

"He has been in the woods more," Mrs Wilkins agreed. "Maybe three of us should go by different routes."

Commander Hoag thought a minute. He stepped to the map. "Is either of these mountains coral?" he asked.

"We don't know," Mr Wilkins answered.

"Pearlstein! Could a man tell if a mountain was coral? How far would he have to dig?"

"I should say . . . well, five feet, sir. In three different places. That's a minimum sample."

Commander Hoag turned to Mr Heskwith. "Would you be willing to risk it?" he asked.

"Of course," Heskwith replied. It was agreed upon.

I was given the job of selecting from volunteers ten enlisted men to make the trip. All one hot afternoon I sat in a little office and watched the faces of brave men who were willing to risk the landing on Konora. There was no clue to their coming, no pattern which directed these particular men to apply. I saw forty-odd men that day and would have been glad to lead any of them on a landing party.

They had but one thing in common. Each man, as he came in to see me, fingered his hat and looked foolish. Almost all of them said something like, "I hear you got a job," or "What's this about a job?" I have since learned that when the Japs want volunteers for something unduly risky, their officers rise and shout at the men about ancestors, emperors, and glory. In the SeaBees, at least, you sort of pass the word around, and pretty soon forty guys come ambling in with their hats in their hands, nervous-like.

Married men I rejected, although I did not doubt that some of them had ample reason to want to try their luck on Konora. Very young boys I turned down too. The first man I accepted was Luther Billis, who knew native tongues and who was born to die on some island like Konora. The gold ring in his left ear danced as he mumbled something about liking to have a kid named Hyman go along. I told him to go get Hyman. A thin Jewish boy, scared to death, appeared. I accepted him, too. The other eight were average, unimpressive, American young men. It would be fashionable, I suppose, to say that I had selected ten of America's "little people" for an adventure against the Japs. But when a fellow crawls ashore on Konora at night to dig three holes, five feet deep, he's not "little people." He's damned big, brother!

As soon as the group was dispatched, Commander Hoag and his staff seemingly forgot all about them. Mr and Mrs Wilkins were sent back to Intelligence. In their place Admiral Kester's leading aviation assistants were called in. Commander Hoag was tough with them.

"I want plenty of air cover on this job," he said briskly as I took notes. "And I want it to be air cover. No stunting around. I don't want the men distracted by a lot of wild men up in the air. And under no circumstances are your men to attempt landings on the airstrip until I give the word." The aviators smiled at one another.

"An aviator's no good if he's not tough," one of them observed.

"Right! Same goes for SeaBees. But tell them to save their stuff for the Nips. Now, what do you think of this? You men are the doctors. Tell me if it's possible. Let's have a constant patrol of New Zealanders in *P-40*s for low cover. They like those heavy planes and do a good clean-up job with them. Give us some *F6F*s or *F4U*s for high cover. And send some *TBF*s out every morning, noon, and night at least two hundred miles."

"You'll tip your hand, Commander," an aviator observed.

"You're right. But the Nips will know we're on the move the minute we hit Konora. Can't help it. So here's what we'll do! We'll send the *TBF*s in three directions, Kuralei, Truk, and Rabaul."

Problems of air cover were settled. Then Logistics men appeared and said what ships we could have and when. Oil tankers were dispatched from San Diego to make rendezvous three weeks later. Commissary men discussed problems of food, and gradually the armada formed. On the day we finished preparations, eighteen bombers plastered Konora. The island was under fire from then on. It knew no respite. And from all parts of the Pacific, Japan rushed what aid it could. Those Jap officers who had smugly advised against building a fighter strip at Konora—since it would never be attacked—kept their mouths shut and wondered.

Finally Commander Hoag's staff moved its equipment and maps on board a liberty ship. That night, as we mulled over our plans, Mr Heskwith and Luther Billis returned from their expedition. Billis was resplendent in tattoos and bracelets. He looked fine in the ship's swaying light. Mr Heskwith was thin, rumpled, reticent.

"We had no trouble," the Australian said quietly. "It was most uneventful."

"Was there a ravine?" Lieut. Pearlstein asked eagerly.

"A deep one," Mr Heskwith replied. "Runs due north and south. Two small streams filter into it."

"How deep? At this point?" Hoag demanded.

Mr Heskwith deferred to Billis. The jangling SeaBee stepped forward and grinned. "Not more than twenty feet," he said.

"And how wide?"

"Thirty yards, maybe," Billis answered. He looked at the Australian.

"Not more," Mr Heskwith agreed.

"And the two mountains?" Hoag inquired.

"The hills?" Heskwith repeated. "We could not get to that one. We don't know. We were able to dig only one hole on this one. It was late."

"But was it coral?"

"Yes."

Billis interrupted. "We got coral, but it was deeper down than any hills around here. Lots."

"But it was coral?"

"Yes, sir!"

Commander Hoag thanked the men and dismissed them. He smiled when he saw Billis clap a huge hand over Mr Heskwith's frail shoulder. He heard Billis whispering: "Guess we told them what they wanted to know, eh, buddy?"

Hoag turned and faced his officers. "There is a considerable gully there. Don't call it a ravine. We assume this hill is coral. Probably three feet of loam over it. All right! We're taking chances. We lost on one and gained on the other. Got a gully and the coral to fill it with, Pearlstein. We'll give you all of 1416, and the heavy trucks. You'll beat a road directly to that hill. Don't stop for anything. Food, huts, gasoline. Nothing. Rip the loam off and move the hill over to here!" He indicated the gully. Before anyone could speak, he barked out eight or ten additional orders. Then he dismissed the men. When they were gone he slumped down in a chair.

"I don't know what we'd have done if there had been a

ravine and no coral!" he said. "I guess God takes care of Americans and SeaBees."

On the way north I got to know Commander Hoag fairly well. He was an engaging man. The finest officer I ever knew. The fact that he was not a regular Navy man kept him from certain supercilious traits of caution that one expects in Annapolis graduates. Hoag was an enterprising man and a hard worker. On the other hand, his social position in civilian life was such that he had acquired those graces of behaviour which mark the true naval officer and distinguish him from men of the other services.

Hoag's men idolized him and told all sorts of silly stories about things he had done. Even his officers, who lived with him daily, revered him and accepted his judgement as almost infallible. I got a sample of that judgement when he confided to me why he had given Pearlstein the job of filling the gully.

"You see," he said thoughtfully, as he watched the Coral Sea, "Pearlstein was right. By shrewd deductions that were available to all of us, he concluded that there must be a gully there. Then he stuck his neck way out and argued with me about it. He was argued down. Or, if you wish, I threw my rank at him. Then it turns out that there really is a gully there. So the logical thing to do is to give it to him to take care of. You watch how he goes about it! He'll steam and swear and curse, but all the time he'll love that gully. Proved he was right and the old man was a damned fool! I'll bet that Pearlstein will fill that hole in a new world's record. But how he'll bitch!"

From time to time on the trip I would hear Pearlstein muttering to himself. "Of all the silly places to build an airstrip! I *told* them there was a gully there!" When he got his special group together to lay plans for their assault on the coral hills, he confided to them, "We've got a mammoth job to do. Biggest job the SeaBees have tackled in the South Pacific. We've got to move a mountain in less than fifteen days. I kept telling them there was a big hole there. Any guy could see there'd have to be. But I think we're the team that can fill it up!''

It seemed to me, as I listened to the various officers talking to their detachments, that each man in that battalion had generated a personal hatred for Konora and everything related to the airstrip. Men in charge of heavy equipment kicked it and cursed it while they lovingly worked upon it in the ships' holds. Luther Billis, who was in charge of trucks and bulldozers, was sure they were the worst in the Navy. "Look at them damn things!" he would moan. "They expect me to move a mountain with them. There ain't a good differential in the bunch. But I guess we'll do it!''

At Guadalcanal two experts came aboard our liberty ship. They carried papers and conferred with the Commander in hush-hush sessions. Finally he called us in. One of the men was a commander and the other a civilian in military uniform. Hoag introduced them and spoke briefly. "Gentlemen," he began, "I have good news and bad news for you. Bad news first. We are going to have to re-plan our entire layout. We've got to dredge our coral from the inner shoreline of the knee, right here. Got to get enough live coral to cover the airstrip. You gentlemen will be expected to lay plans accordingly. The good news is that if we use live coral for runways, they will be better than any in the area. Because we can keep that coral living with plenty of salt water every day. And live coral binds better, is more resilient, and won't throw dust!''

A storm of chatter greeted this announcement. Was the old man nuts? Hoag let his energetic men damn the project and then called on the civilian to explain. "It's preposterous, I know," the expert said. "But we have more than proved

219

that coral will stay alive for some days if watered daily with fresh sea-water. If the organisms remain living, they grow ever so slightly and fill the interstices that otherwise develop. Your airplane then lands upon a living, resilient mat. All you have to do is to keep feeding it sea-water."

The visiting commander then took over. "We decided to make the experiment . . . No, it's not an experiment! It's a fact! But we decided to do it for the first time in a big way on Konora. We've a ship off Lunga Point with special dredging equipment. And we have four massive, glass-lined milk trucks with rust-proof spigots for watering. We've put it to Commander Hoag. We're not forcing this on him. Meeting his schedule is still of paramount importance. But you'll have a much better job if you use this new method."

There was a long silence. Then an ensign spoke up. "You dig the coral from under the water?"

"Yes, sir."

"Special equipment?"

"Yes, sir."

"Gasoline or diesel?"

"Diesel." There were no more questions. Hoag thought a moment, studied the map. He was going to make some comment, but thought better of it. "That's all, gentlemen," he said dryly. "You know what this means. Run your roads down here. Oh yes! That's what I was trying to remember. You'll have to run trucking lines to each end of the airstrip. Pearlstein tells me it will take at least twelve days to make his fill. We'll work both ends and meet in the middle."

The visitors left, and that night our ship started north. Behind us trailed the new ship with its strange equipment. I noticed particularly that the officers no longer ridiculed the idea of live coral. "That guy may have something," one of the wiriest of the young men said. They did, however, complain bitterly about the extra work. To hear them talk you would have thought it quite impossible to build an extra road on Konora.

But all arguments ceased when five troop-transports of Marines met us one morning. It was a solemn moment when they hove in sight. We knew what these ships were, and that our lives and fortunes depended on those Leathernecks. At such moments a bond is established that no subsequent hardships can ever break. From that moment, the Marines in those ships were our friends. We would see none of them until we hit the beaches they had won for us, and some of them would never speak to us, lying upon the shores . . . Those Marines were our friends.

Two days later heavy warships swung into line, and next morning we were at Konora. All day our forces alternated between aerial bombardment and naval shell-fire. It was awe-inspiring to witness the split-second timing. It was sickening to imagine oneself on that shore. I recall my thoughts distinctly—"A long time ago the Japs came down like this and shelled us on Guadal. Strange, but they'll never do that again!"

In the night, great shells whined through the air, and at 0400 we saw the first Marines go ashore. The landing was neither tragic nor easy. It was a routine Marine landing, with some casualties but with planned success. At four-thirty in the afternoon the first SeaBee detachments went ashore. They were to throw up huts and a camp area. That night they were attacked by Japs and four SeaBees were killed.

At daybreak our first heavy lighters headed for shore. They carried Luther Billis, a dozen bulldozers, and Lieut. Pearlstein's men. I saw them as they hit the shore. In three minutes a bulldozer edged on to the sand and started for the brush. In four minutes more a tree was toppling. All that day Pearlstein and his men drove madly for the coral hill. It

221

took two companies of Marines to protect them. At sunset that day Pearlstein was half-way to the hill. His men worked all night, with ghostly flares lighting their way, and two of them were wounded.

One of the wounded men was Luther Billis, who insisted upon being in the front lines. He suffered a superficial flesh wound, but the corpsman who treated him was a bit of a wag. He had with him a home-made purple heart, which he pinned on Billis's pants, since the "big-dealer" could not be made to wear a shirt. Next morning Billis barged into the head of the line where they were serving coffee. "I'm a bloody hero!" he bellowed. "Special privileges." He then proceeded to revile the Marine Corps in frightful language. "They didn't protect me!" he roared. "Ran away when the going got tough!" The Marines, who had taken a liking to the fat nomad, countered with an improvised sign painted with mercurochrome: *Billis Boulevard.* The name still stands on Konora.

There were more Japs on the island than we had anticipated. It would be incorrect to say that the SeaBees had to stop operations in order to fight the yellow devils, but each working party had to have infantry protection. If Marines were not available, SeaBees had to provide their own snipers. Artisans forty years old who had expected to work in Pearl Harbour and sleep between sheets, swore, bitched, and grabbed rifles. I doubt if the SeaBees altogether killed two Japs. But they sure used up a pile of ammunition!

By the third day the Marines had a perimeter safely established. That night at seven o'clock Pearlstein reached his first objective: the coral hill. Billis and some rowdies set up a terrific small-arms barrage in honour of the event. The Marine commandant sent a special runner to see what had happened. He was furious when he heard the explanation, and called for Hoag.

"I won't have your men firing that way!" he snapped. "Yes, sir!" Hoag replied briskly. But he said nothing to anybody about the rebuke.

On the fifth day, with tractors and bulldozers making a shambles of Konora, I went to see how the live coral project was developing. In the lagoon, within the protecting angle of the bend, an energetic crew had established a dredging process. They had half a dozen massive steel maws which they sank on to the coral bottom. The maws were then slowly dragged on to the beach, where a tripping device threw the collected coral into piles. As I watched, a giant steam shovel came slowly out of the jungle behind me, like a pterodactyl. It moved with horrible slowness, crunchingness, and grinding. It took up a position on the beach from which it could scoop up the live coral. Trucks were ready waiting for their first loads.

"Would you like to see what we're getting?" an officer asked me. I went with him to the furthest dredge. We waited until a fresh batch was hauled in and tripped. Then we stepped forward to examine the catch.

In the crushed pile at our feet we saw a wonderland. Coral grows like an underwater bush. It is of many colours, ranging from exquisite pastel greens to violent, bleeding reds. There is blue coral, orange, purple, grey, amethyst, and even now and then a bush of stark, black coral. Like human beings, it grows white as it approaches death.

The officer broke off a branch of living coral and handed it to me. It was purple, and was composed of a stony base, already calcified. Next to that was a pulpy, mineral segment, pale white in colour. The extreme tip was almost purely vegetable. It exuded a sticky milk which smelled noxiously. Over all were suction caps like those on the tentacles of an octopus. They were potential tips which had not matured.

It was impossible to believe that this tiny organism and its stony shell had raised the island on which we stood and was at that moment raising thousands of new islands throughout the Pacific, most of which would never break the waves but would remain subterranean palaces of rare wonder. It was equally difficult to believe that the evil-smelling, whitish milk would shortly go to work for the SeaBees!

The days dragged on. I saw little of Pearlstein, but I heard that he had run into all sorts of trouble. On the seventh day he got more than his share. A Jap bomber came over, one of the nine that tried, and laid an egg right on Pearlstein's steam shovel. Killed two men and wounded one. The shovel was wrecked. I was sent up to see what I could do to get him another.

Pearlstein had tears in his eyes. "Goddam it all," he said. "You try and try! Then something like this happens!" He surveyed the ruined shovel. I knew little about machinery, but it seemed to me that the shovel was not too badly wrecked. After the dead bodies were removed we studied what was left of the machinery.

"Billis?" I asked. "Couldn't you run that without the controls? I mean, couldn't you counterweight it with a tractor? The boom still works."

Billis and his men looked at the complex job I had set them. "It could be done, sir," the dirty fat man said. "But it would take . . ."

"Let's start right away!" Pearlstein cried when he perceived what might be done. "Look, fellows. All we'll have to do is bulldoze the coral over here. We won't move the shovel again. Let's see what we can do!" I left Pearlstein, bare to the waist, high up the boom of the shovel, loosening some bolts.

At night we could hear shots in the jungle. Some men swore that Japs had infiltrated the lines and stolen food. Others were afraid to sleep. But gradually the lines were pushed back and back. There were now apparently no Japs within the knee. And Marines had landed at each tip, so that two tightly compressing pockets were all that remained for the yellow men.

On the eighth day New Zealanders put on a terrific air show for us. Two squadrons of Jap fighters came over and shot us up fairly badly. Eight men were wounded and three killed. But the New Zealanders, in their crushing style, drove the Japs into the sea. Everybody stopped work, of course, and we counted seven Jap planes crash either in the sea or on Konora. One wild Jap tried to crash on the airstrip but instead crashed into the coral hill, where he completely demolished Pearlstein's improvised shovel and injured four men.

That night we had a hurried meeting. It was decided that the steam shovel at the live coral pits should be moved to the hillside. For if the gully was not filled, it mattered little whether live coral were available or not. Therefore, at 2100 a strange procession set out across Konora. Billis rode in front on his favourite bulldozer. Any tree that might hinder passage of the steam shovel was knocked over. It was astonishing to me how easily a huge tree could be uprooted and shoved aside. Billis later told me it was because the roots had nowhere to go. They could not penetrate the coral.

Slowly, with horrible noises, we inched our way along the jungle trails. At one place water had collected and the bulldozer bogged down. We waited an hour till another came to haul it free. Then together, like monsters, they shoved tree after tree into that depression. Slowly, the giant shovel edged its way on to the bridge, into the middle and across. By that time Billis was on ahead, knocking down a banyan.

At the foot of the hill six tractors threw down cables and inched the shovel up the incline. At dawn it was in place. At

dawn a smart young ensign at the live coral pits had completed a platform arrangement whereby dredge loads could be emptied directly into trucks. At dawn work went on.

All this time Commander Hoag was a great, restless reservoir of energy. He worked with all hands, helped to build the platform at the live coral pits. He was constantly with the wounded and had to bite his lip when he watched a fine young friend lose a leg. But mostly he was on the airstrip. It progressed so slowly. God, it crawled along!

Starting from either end two companies with tractors had knocked down all the trees and pushed them into the southern extremities of the ravine. Hoag would not permit trees to be used as filler for the airstrip itself. That must be coral. Next the foot or so of topsoil was bulldozed away to block the highest section of the ravine. In this way the normal strip of rain-water was diverted into the ocean without crossing the strip. That left a long, fine stretch of native coral rock, broken in the middle by the ravine.

Again starting from either end, bulldozers slowly pushed the top layer of coral toward the ravine. By that time Pearlstein's trucks were beginning to roll. Coral from the hillside rumbled to the airstrip twenty-four hours a day. At the same time, live coral from the sea was hauled to the two ends. Six steam rollers worked back and forth constantly. At the north side of the strip, a company of carpenters built a control-tower. Electricians had already completed two identical power-plants and were installing floodlights. From then on, day and night were the same on Konora.

As yet no one but Hoag was sure the airstrip would be completed on time. With his permission I sent Admiral Kester a message telling him to schedule bombers for the field at the appointed time. On the sixteenth day the bombers would be there! We wondered if there would be a field for them to land on.

226

At this point a wonderful thing happened. Luther Billis disappeared for two days! We thought he was dead, lying somewhere in the bush, but on the evening of the second day he appeared in camp with two Japanese Samurai swords. He gave one to Commander Hoag just before he was thrown into the brig. After dinner the Marine commandant came over and asked if Commander Hoag wouldn't please drop charges against Billis. It seems some Marines had been saying how tough they were, and Billis listened for a while and then bet them that he could go down the west leg and get himself a sword, which they wouldn't be able to do down the east leg. It seems that Billis had won, and it wasn't quite right, the Marines thought, that he should be punished. Besides, he told them where the Jap camp was.

Commander Hoag thought for a while and released the "big dealer". Billis told us all about it. Seems his old lady ran a news-stand in Pittsburg. He sent her a Jap ear from Guadal and she hung it up in the store. People came from all over to see it. He'd promised her a Jap sword, too, so he thought he'd better be getting one. He was going to send it to Pittsburg. What Commander Hoag did with his was the old man's worry.

That night we had torrential rains. Floodlights on the fields silhouetted men working in water up to their ankles. The gully, thank heavens, held. The dirt and trees had really diverted the rains. In the morning there was hardly any sign of water. Men who had slept through the deluge refused to believe there had been one.

By this time the milk trucks were running. The drivers were subjected to merciless ridicule, especially one who forgot to turn the spigots off and arrived with an empty truck. That day one of Pearlstein's drivers, coming down the hill at a great clip, overturned and was killed. The truck was ruined beyond repair. A SeaBee was then stationed at the dangerous spot to warn drivers to keep their speed down, but next day another truck went right on over. The driver merely broke both legs, but the truck was wrecked.

"I can't make them slow down!" Lieut. Pearlstein objected. "They know the schedule!"

The Japs knew the schedule, too, apparently, for they started sending large numbers of bombers over at night plus four or five solitary nuisance raiders. "We'll have to turn off the lights," Commander Hoag reluctantly decided. But when work lagged way behind schedule, he announced that the twenty-four hour shift would be resumed.

Night fighters were sent to help us. They knocked down two Jap bombers the first night we kept the lights on, and from then on not one SeaBee was killed by bombing. Men working on the strip could not praise our aviators enough. It was a good feeling, having Yank fighters upstairs.

On the morning of the fifteenth day Lieut. Pearlstein, gaunt, unshaven, and nervous, reported to Commander Hoag. "You can finish the airstrip, sir. The gully won't take any more coral." Hoag said nothing. Held out his hand and shook Pearlstein's warmly. As the lieutenant was about to leave, Hoag made a suggestion.

"Why don't you sleep on one of the ships tonight? You could use some rest."

That afternoon a strange incident occurred, one which I have thought about time and again. An *S.B.D.* flying medium-high cover tangled with a Jap intruder and shot it down. The Nip went flaming into the sea. They always tried to hit the runway, but this one failed. Before he took his last long fling, however, he did manage to pepper the *S.B.D.* and the pilot had a difficult choice to make. He could try a water landing, or he could head for the uncompleted field.

"Clear the middle of the strip!" he called to the tower. "I'm coming in."

When his intention was apparent, Commander Hoag became almost insane with fury. "Stop that plane!" he shouted to the operations officer, but the officer ignored him. Hoag had no right to give such an order. Trembling, he watched the *S.B.D.* approach, swerve badly when the unfilled portion loomed ahead, and slide past on a thin strip that had been filled.

The enlisted men cheered wildly at the superb landing. They stormed around the plane. Brandishing his revolver, Commander Hoag shouted that everyone was to go back to work immediately. He was like a wild man.

From the cockpit of the *S.B.D.* climbed Bus Adams. He grinned at me and reached for the commander's hand. "You had no right to land here!" Hoag stormed. "I expressly forbade it. Look at the mess you've made!"

Adams looked at me and tapped his forehead. "No, no!" I wigwagged.

"Get than plane off the strip at once. Shove it off if you have to!" Hoag shouted. He refused to speak further to Bus. When the plane had been pulled into a revetment by men who wondered how Bus had ever brought her in, Commander Hoag stormed from the field.

That night he came to see Bus and me. He was worn and haggard. He looked like an old man. He would not sit with us, nor would he permit us to interrupt his apology. "For six weeks I've done nothing but plan and fight to have this strip ready for bombers on the sixteenth day. We've had to fight rains, accidents, changes, and every damned thing else. Then this afternoon, you land. I guess my nerves must have snapped. You see, sir," he said, addressing Bus, "we've lost a lot of men on this strip. Every foot has been paid for. It's not to be misused lightly."

He left us. I don't know whether he got any sleep that night, for next morning, still haggard, he was up and waiting at 0700. It was the sixteenth day, and bombers were due from Guadalcanal and Munda. The gully was filled. On the sea-shore trucks were idle, and upon the hill the great shovel rested. On the legs of the island desperate Japs connived at ways to outwit Marines. And all over the Pacific tremendous preparations for taking Kuralei were in motion. It was a solemn day.

Then, from the east, specks appeared. They were! They were the bombers! In the radio-tower orders were issued. The specks increased in size geometrically, fabulously. In grandeur they buzzed the field, finest in the Pacific. Then they formed a traffic circle and the first bomber to land on Konora roared in. The strip was springy, fine, borne up by living coral, and the determination of free men. At this precise moment three Japanese soldiers who had been lurking near the field in starving silence dashed from their cover and tried to charge the bomber.

Two were shot by Marines, but the third plunged madly on. Screaming, wild dishevelled, his eyes popping from his horrible head, this primitive, indecent thing surged on like his inscrutable ancestors. Clutching a grenade to his belly and shouting *Banzai*, he threw himself forward and knocked Commander Hoag to the ground.

The grenade exploded! It took the mad Jap to a heaven reserved for the *hara-kiri* boys. It took Commander Hoag, a free man, a man of thought and dignity, a man for whom other men would die . . . This horrible, indecent, meaningless act of madness took Hoag to his death. But above, the bombers wheeled and came in for their landings, whence they would proceed to Kuralei, to Manila, and to Tokyo.

Mij Airborne

GAVIN MAXWELL

A cock, a sheep and a duck taken up on an eighteenth century balloon ascent. A pig flown in an aircraft in 1909—just to test out the saying "If pigs might fly". Laika, the Russian dog orbiting in space—not to mention various monkeys and mice. So airborne animals are no novelty and nowadays they have their own specially equipped aircraft and trained air-attendants. Here, from Ring of Bright Water, *the author describes how he got his famous otter-hero home from the Middle East.*

Then began a journey the like of which I hope I shall never know again. I sat in the back of the car with the box beside me as the Arab driver tore through the streets of Basra like a ricocheting bullet. Donkeys reared, bicycles swerved wildly, out in the suburbs goats stampeded and poultry found un-guessed powers of flight. Mij cried unceasingly in the box, and both of us were hurled to and fro and up and down like drinks in a cocktail shaker. Exactly as we drew to a screeching stop before the airport entrance I heard a splintering sound from the box beside me, and saw Mij's nose force up the lid. He had summoned all the strength in his small body and torn one of the hinges clean out of the wood.

The aircraft was waiting to take off; as I was rushed through the customs by infuriated officials I was trying all the time to hold down the lid of the box with one hand, and

231

with the other, using a screwdriver purloined from the driver, to force back the screws into the splintered wood. But I knew that it could be no more than a temporary measure at best, and my imagination boggled at the thought of the next twenty-four hours.

It was perhaps my only stroke of fortune that the seat booked for me was at the extreme front of the aircraft, so that I had a bulkhead before me instead of another seat. The other passengers, a remarkable cross-section of the Orient and Occident, stared curiously as the dishevelled late arrival struggled up the gangway with a horrifying vocal Charles-Addams-like box, and knowing for just what a short time it could remain closed I was on tenterhooks to see what manner of passenger would be my immediate neighbour. I had a moment of real dismay when I saw her to be an elegantly dressed American woman in early middle age. Such a one, I thought, would have little sympathy or tolerance for the draggled and dirty otter cub that would so soon and so inevitably be in her midst. For the moment the lid held, and as I sat down and fastened my safety belt there seemed to be a temporary silence from within.

The port engines roared, and then the starboard, and the aircraft trembled and teetered against the tug of her propellers. Then we were taxiing out to take off, and I reflected that whatever was to happen now there could be no escape from it, for the next stop was Cairo. Ten minutes later we were flying westwards over the great marshes that had been Mij's home, and peering downward into the dark I could see the glint of their waters beneath the moon.

I had brought a brief-case full of old newspapers and a parcel of fish and with these scant resources I prepared myself to withstand a siege. I arranged newspapers to cover all the floor around my feet, rang for the air hostess, and asked her to keep the fish in a cool place. I have retained the most

profound admiration for that air hostess, and in subsequent
sieges and skirmishes with otters in public places I have
found my thoughts turning towards her as a man's mind
turns to water in desert wastes. She was the very queen of
her kind. I took her into my confidence; the events of the
last half-hour together with the prospect of the next twenty-
four had shaken my equilibrium a little, and I daresay I was
not too coherent, but she took it all in her graceful sheer nylon
stride, and she received the ill-wrapped fish into her shapely
hands as though I were travelling royalty depositing a jewel-
case with her for safe keeping. Then she turned and spoke
with her countrywoman on my left. Would I not prefer, she
then enquired, to have my pet on my knee? The animal
would surely feel happier there, and my neighbour had no
objection. I could have kissed her hand in the depth of my
gratitude. But not knowing otters, I was quite unprepared
for what followed.

I unlocked the padlock and opened the lid, and Mij was
out like a flash. He dodged my fumbling hands with an eel-
like wriggle and disappeared at high speed down the fuselage
of the aircraft. As I tried to get into the gangway I could
follow his progress among the passengers by a wave of
disturbance amongst them not unlike that caused by the
passage of a stoat through a hen-run. There were squawks
and shrieks and a flapping of travelling-coats, and half-way
down the fuselage a woman stood up on her seat, screaming
out, "A rat! A rat!" Then the air hostess reached her, and
within a matter of seconds she was seated again and smiling
benignly. That goddess, I believe, could have controlled a
panic-stricken crowd single-handed.

By now I was in the gangway myself and, catching sight
of Mij's tail disappearing beneath the legs of a portly white-
turbanned Indian, I tried a flying tackle, landing flat on my
face. I missed Mij's tail, but found myself clasping the

sandalled foot of the Indian's female companion; further-more my face was inexplicably covered in curry. I staggered up, babbling inarticulate apology, and the Indian gave me a long silent stare, so utterly expressionless that even in my hypersensitive mood I could deduce from it no meaning whatsoever. I was, however, glad to observe that something, possibly the curry, had won over the bulk of my fellow passengers, and that they were regarding me now as a harmless clown rather than as a dangerous lunatic. The air hostess stepped into the breach once more.

"Perhaps," she said with the most charming smile, "it would be better if you resumed your seat, and I will find the animal and bring it to you." She would probably have said the same had Mij been an escaped rogue elephant. I explained that Mij, being lost and frightened, might bite a stranger, but she did not think so. I returned to my seat.

I heard the ripple of flight and pursuit behind me, but I could see little. I was craning my neck back over the seat trying to follow the hunt when suddenly I heard from my feet a distressed chitter of recognition and welcome, and Mij bounded on my knee and began to nuzzle my face and neck. In all the strange world of the aircraft I was the only familiar thing to be found, and in that first spontaneous return was sown the seed of the absolute trust that he accorded me for the rest of his life.

Otters are extremely bad at doing nothing. That is to say that they cannot, as a dog does, lie still and awake; they are either asleep or entirely absorbed in play or other activity. If there is no acceptable toy, or if they are in a mood of frustra-tion, they will, apparently with the utmost good humour, set about laying the land waste. There is, I am convinced, something positively provoking to an otter about order and tidiness in any form, and the greater the state of confusion that they can create about them the more contented they feel, though it must be said that this aspect of an otter's behaviour is certainly due to its intense inquisitiveness. An otter must find out everything and have a hand in everything; but most of all he must know what lies inside any man-made container or beyond any man-made obstruction. This combined with an uncanny mechanical sense of how to get things open makes it much safer to remove valuables rather than to challenge the otter's ingenuity by inventive obstructions. But in those days I had all this to learn.

We had been flying for perhaps five hours, and must, I thought, be nearing Cairo, when one of those moods descended on Mij. It opened comparatively innocuously, with an assault upon the newspapers spread carefully round my feet, and in a minute or two the place looked like a street upon which royalty has been given a ticker-tape welcome. Then he turned his attentions to the box, where his sleeping compartment was filled with fine wood-shavings. First he put his head and shoulders in and began to throw these out backwards at enormous speed; then he got in bodily and lay on his back, using all four feet in a pedalling motion to hoist out the remainder. I was doing my best to cope with the litter, but it was like a ship's pumps working against a leak too great for them, and I was hopelessly behind in the race when he turned his attention to my neighbour's canvas Trans-World travel bag on the floor beside him. The zipper gave him pause for no more than seconds; by chance, in all likelihood, he yanked it back and was in head first, throwing out magazines, handkerchiefs, gloves, bottles of pills, tins of ear-plugs and all the personal paraphernalia of long-distance air travel. My neighbour was sleeping profoundly; I managed, unobserved, to haul Mij out by the tail and cram the things back somehow. I hoped that she might leave the aircraft at Cairo, before the outrage was discovered, and to my infinite relief she did so.

Satellite Passage

THEODORE L. THOMAS

> "*Schoolboys at Kettering, Northants, who have made a hobby of tracking spaceshots, announced that the Soviet Union's latest rehearsal for the space link-up with an American* Apollo *craft had ended successfully after six days in earth orbit. The* Soyuz-16 *spacecraft, modernized to meet requirements of the U.S.–Soviet joint project, functioned normally at all stages.*" *This news item is in pleasant contrast with the space-war atmosphere evident at one point in this 1958 story.*

The three men bent over the chart and once again computed the orbit. It was quiet in the satellite, a busy quiet broken by the click of seeking microswitches and the gentle purr of smooth-running motors. The deep, pulsing throb of the air-conditioner had stopped; the satellite was in the Earth's shadow and there was no need for cooling the interior.

"Well," said Morgan, "it checks. We'll pass within fifty feet of the other satellite. Too close. Think we ought to move?"

Kaufman looked at him and did not speak. McNary glanced up and snorted. Morgan nodded. He said, "That's right. If there's any moving to be done, let them do it." He felt a curious, nascent emotion, a blend of anger and exhilaration—very faint now, just strong enough to be recognizable. The pencil snapped in his fingers, and he stared at it, and smiled.

Kaufman said, "Any way we can reline this a little? Fifty feet cuts it kind of close."

They were silent, and the murmuring of machinery filled the cramped room. "How's this?" said McNary. "Wait till we see the other satellite, take a couple of readings on it, and compute the orbit again. We'd have about five minutes to make the calculations. Morgan here can do it in less than that. Then we'd know if we're on a collision course."

Morgan nodded. "We could do it that way." He studied the chart in front of him. "The only thing, those boys on the other satellite will see what we're doing. They'll know we're afraid of a collision. They'll radio it down to Earth, and— you know the Russian mind—we'll lose face."

"That's so bad?" asked Kaufman.

Morgan stared at the chart. He answered softly. "Yes, I think it is. The Russians will milk it dry if we make any move to get our satellite out of the way of theirs. We can't do that to our people."

McNary nodded. Kaufman said, "Agree. Just wanted to throw it out. We stay put. We hit, we hit."

The other two looked at Kaufman. The abrupt dismissal of a serious problem was characteristic of the little astronomer; Kaufman wasted no time with second guesses. A decision made was a fact accomplished; it was over.

Morgan glanced at McNary to see how he was taking it. McNary, now, big as he was, was a worrier. He stood ready to change his mind at any time, whenever some new alternative looked better. Only the soundness of his judgement prevented his being putty in any strong hands. He was a meteorologist, and a good one.

"You know," McNary said, "I still can't quite believe it. Two satellites, one pole-to-pole, the other equatorial, both having apogees and perigees of different elevations—yet they wind up on what amounts to a collision course."

THEODORE L. THOMAS

Morgan said, "That's what regression will do for you. But we haven't got any time for that; we've got to think this out. Let's see, they'll be coming up from below us at passage. Can we make anything of that?"

There was silence while the three men considered it. Morgan's mind was focused on the thing that was about to happen; but wisps of memory intruded. Faintly he could hear the waves, smell the bite in the salt sea air. A man who had sailed a thirty-two-foot ketch alone into every corner of the globe never thereafter quite lost the sound of the sea in his ear. And the struggle, the duel, the strain of outguessing the implacable elements, there was a test of a man . . .

"Better be outside in any case," said Kaufman. "Suited up and outside. They'll see us, and know we intend to do nothing to avoid collision. Also, we'll be in a better position to cope with anything that comes along, if we're in the suits."

Morgan and McNary nodded, and again there was talk. They discussed the desirability of radio communication with the other satellite, and decided against it. To keep their own conversations private, they agreed to use telephone communication instead of radio. When the discussion trailed off, Kaufman said, "Be some picture, if we have the course computed right. We stand there and wave at 'em as they go by."

Morgan tried to see it in his mind: three men standing on a long, slim tube, and waving at three men on another. The first rocket passage, and me waving. And then Morgan remembered something, and the image changed.

He saw flimsy, awkward planes sputtering past each other on the morning's mission. The pilots, detached observers, non-combatants really, waved at each other as the rickety planes passed. Kindred souls they were, high above the walks of normal men. So they waved . . . for a while. Morgan said, "Do you suppose they'll try anything?"

"Like what?" said Kaufman.

"Like knocking us out of orbit if they can. Like shooting at us if they have a gun. Like throwing something at us, if they've got nothing better to do."

"My God," said McNary, "you think they might have brought a gun up here?"

Morgan began examining the interior of the tiny cabin. Slowly he turned his head, looking at one piece of equipment after another, visualizing what was packed away under it and behind it. To the right of the radio was the spacesuit locker, and his glance lingered there. He reached over, opened the door and slipped a hand under the suits packed in the locker. For a moment he fumbled and then he sat back holding an oxygen flask in his hand. He hefted the small steel flask and looked at Kaufman. "Can you think of anything better than this for throwing?"

Kaufman took it and hefted it in his turn, and passed it to McNary. McNary did the same and then carefully held it in front of him and took his hand away. The flask remained poised in mid-air, motionless. Kaufman shook his head and said, "I can't think of anything better. It's got good mass, fits the hand well. It'll do."

Morgan said, "Another thing. We clip extra flasks to our belts and they look like part of the standard equipment. It won't be obvious that we're carrying something we can throw."

McNary gently pushed the flask towards Morgan, who caught it and replaced it. McNeary said, "I used to throw a hot pass at Berkeley. I wonder how the old arm is."

The discussion went on. At one point the radio came to life and Kaufman had a lengthy conversation with one of the control points on the surface of the planet below. They talked in code. It was agreed that the American satellite should not move to make room for the other, and this information was carefully leaked so the Russians would be aware of the decision.

The only difficulty was that the Russians also leaked the information that their satellite would not move, either.

A final check of the two orbits revealed no change. Kaufman switched off the set.

"That", he said, "is the whole of it."

"They're leaving us pretty much on our own," said McNary.

"Couldn't be any other way," Morgan answered. "We're the ones at the scene. Besides"—he smiled his tight smile—"they trust us."

Kaufman snorted. "Ought to. They went to enough trouble to pick us."

McNary looked at the chronometer and said, "Three-quarters of an hour to passage. We'd better suit up."

Morgan nodded and reached again into the suit locker. The top suit was McNary's, and as he worked his way into it, Morgan and Kaufman pressed against the walls to give him room. Kaufman was next, and then Morgan. They set out the helmets, and while Kaufman and McNary made a final check of the equipment, Morgan took several sights to verify their position.

"Luck," said Kaufman, and dropped his helmet over his head. The others followed and they all went through the air-sealing check-off. They passed the telephone wire around, and tested the circuit. Morgan handed out extra oxygen flasks, three for each. Kaufman waved, squeezed into the air-lock and pulled the hatch closed behind him. McNary went next, then Morgan.

Morgan carefully pulled himself erect alongside the outer hatch and plugged the telephone jack into his helmet. As he straightened, he saw the Earth directly in front of him. It loomed large, visible as a great mass of blackness cutting off the harsh white starshine. The blackness was smudged with irregular patches of orangeish light that marked the cities of Earth.

Morgan became aware that McNary, beside him, was pointing towards the centre of the Earth. Following the line of his finger Morgan could see a slight flicker of light against the blackness; it was so faint that he had to look above it to see it.

"Storm," said McNary. "Just below the Equator. It must be a pip if we can see the lightning through the clouds from here. I've been watching it develop for the last two days."

Morgan stared, and nodded to himself. He knew what it was like down there. The familiar feeling was building up, stronger now as the time to passage drew closer. First the waiting. The sea, restless in expectancy as the waves tossed their hoary manes. The gathering majesty of the elements, reaching, searching, striving . . . And if at the height of the contest the screaming wind snatched up and smothered a defiant roar from a mortal throat, there was none to tell of it.

Then the time came when the forces waned. A slight let-up at first, then another. Soon the toothed and jagged edge of the waves subsided, the hard, side-driven spray and rain assumed a more normal direction.

The man looked after the departing storm, and there was pain in his eyes, longing. Almost, the words rose to his lips, "Come back, I am still here, do not leave me, come back." But the silent supplication went unanswered, and the man was left with a taste of glory gone, with an emptiness that drained the soul. The encounter had ended, the man had won. But the winning was bitter. The hard fight was not hard enough. Somewhere there must be a test sufficient to try the mettle of this man. Somewhere there was a crucible hot enough to float any dross. But where? The man searched and searched, but could not find it.

Morgan turned his head away from the storm and saw that Kaufman and McNary had walked to the top of the satellite. Carefully he turned his body and began placing one foot in front of the other to join them. Yes, he thought, men must always be on top, even if the top is only a state of mind. Here on the outer surface of the satellite, clinging to the metallic skin with shoes of magnetized alloy, there was no top. One direction was the same as another, as with a fly walking on a chandelier. Yet some primordial impulse drove a man to that position which he considered the top, drove him to stand with his feet pointed towards the Earth and his head towards the outer reaches where the stars moved.

Walking under these conditions was difficult, so Morgan moved with care. The feet could easily tread ahead of the man without his knowing it, or they could lag behind. A slight, unthinking motion could detach the shoes from the satellite, leaving the man floating free, unable to return. So Morgan moved with care, keeping the telephone line clear with one hand.

When he reached the others, Morgan stopped and looked around. The sight always gave him pause. It was not pretty; rather, it was harsh and garish like the raucous illumination of a honky-tonk saloon. The black was too black, and the stars burned too white. Everything appeared sharp and hard, with none of the softness seen from the Earth.

Morgan stared, and his lips curled back over his teeth. The anticipation inside him grew greater. No sound and fury here; the menace was of a different sort. Looming, quietly foreboding, it was everywhere.

Morgan leaned back to look overhead, and his lips curled further. This was where it might come, this was the place. Raw space, where a man moved and breathed in momentary peril, where cosmic debris formed arrow-swift reefs on which to founder, where star-born particles travelled at unthinkable speeds out of the macrocosm, seeking some fragile microcosm to shatter.

"Sun." Kaufman's voice echoed tinnily inside the helmet. Morgan brought his head down. There, ahead, a tinge of deep red edged a narrow segment of the black Earth. The red brightened rapidly, and broadened. Morgan reached to one side of his helmet and dropped a filter into place; he continued to stare at the sun.

McNary said, "Ten minutes to passage."

Morgan unhooked one of the oxygen cylinders at his belt and said, "We need some practice. We'd better try throwing one of these now; not much time left." He turned sideways and made several throwing motions with his right hand without releasing the cylinder. "Better lean into it more than you would down below. Well, here goes." He pushed the telephone line clear of his right side and leaned back, raising his right arm. He began to lean forward. When it seemed that he must topple, he snapped his arm down and threw the cylinder. The recoil straightened him neatly, and he stood securely upright. The cylinder shot out and down in a straight line and was quickly lost to sight.

"Very nice," said McNary. "Good timing. I'll keep mine low too. No sense cluttering the orbits up here with any more junk." Carefully McNary leaned back, leaned forward, and threw. The second cylinder followed the first, and McNary kept his footing.

Without speaking Kaufman went though the preliminaries and launched his cylinder. Morgan and McNary watched it speed into the distance. "Shooting stars on Earth tonight," said McNary.

"Quick! I'm off." It was Kaufman.

Morgan and McNary turned to see Kaufman floating several feet above the satellite, and slowly receding. Morgan stepped toward him and scooped up the telephone wire that ran to Kaufman's helmet. Kaufman swung an arm in a circle so that it became entangled in the wire. Morgan carefully drew the wire taut and checked Kaufman's outward motion. Gently, so as not to snap the wire, he slowly reeled him in. McNary grasped Kaufman's shoulders and turned him so that his feet touched the metal shell of the satellite.

McNary chuckled and said, "Why didn't you ride an oxygen cylinder down?"

Kaufman grunted and said, "Oh, sure. I'll leave that to the idiots in the movies; that's the only place a man can ride a cylinder in space." He turned to Morgan. "Thanks. Do as much for you some day."

"Hope you don't have to," Morgan answered. "Look, any throwing to be done better leave it to Mac and me. We can't be fishing anyone back if things get hot."

"Right," said Kaufman, "I'll do what I can to fend off anything they throw at us." He sniffed. "Be simpler if we have a collision."

Morgan was staring to the left. He lifted a hand and pointed. "That it?"

The others squinted in that direction. After a moment they saw the spot of light moving swiftly up and across the black backdrop of the naked sky. "Must be," said Kaufman. "Right time, right place. Must be."

Morgan proudly turned his back on the sun and closed his eyes; he would need his best vision shortly now, and he wanted his pupils dilated as much as possible. "Make anything out yet?" he said.

"No. Little brighter."

Morgan stood without moving. He could feel the heat on his back as his suit seized the radiant energy from the sun and converted it to heat. He grew warmer at the back, yet his front remained cold. The sensation was familiar, and

244

Morgan sought to place it. Yes, that was it—a fire-place. He felt as does a man who stands in a cold room with his back towards a roaring fire. One side toasted, the other side frigid. Funny, the homely sensations, even here.

"Damn face-plate." It was Kaufman. He had scraped the front of his helmet against the outside hatch a week ago. Since then the scratches distracted him every time he wore the helmet.

Morgan waited, and the exultation seethed and bubbled and fumed. "Anything?" he said.

"It's brighter," said McNary. "But—wait a minute, I can make it out. They're outside, the three of them. I can just see them."

It was time. Morgan turned to face the approaching satellite. He raised a hand to shield his face-plate from the sun and carefully opened his eyes. He shifted his hand into the proper position and studied the other satellite.

It was like their own, even to the three men standing on it, except that the three were spaced farther apart.

"Any sign of a rifle or gun?" asked McNary.

"Not that I see," said Morgan. "They're not close enough to tell."

He watched the other satellite grow larger and he tried to judge its course, but it was too far away. Although his eyes were on the satellite his side vision noted the bright-lit Earth below and the stars beyond. A small part of his mind was amused by his own stubborn egocentricity. Knowing well that he was moving and moving fast, he still felt that he stood motionless while the rest of the universe revolved around him. The great globe seemed to be majestically turning under his rooted feet. The harsh brilliances that were the stars seemed to sweep by overhead. And that on-coming satellite, it seemed not to move so much as merely swell in size as he watched.

One of the tiny figures on the other satellite shifted its position towards the others. Sensitive to the smallest detail, Morgan said, "He didn't clear a line when he walked. No telephone. They're on radio. See if we can find the frequency. Mac, take the low. Shorty, the medium. I'll take the high."

Morgan reached to his helmet and began turning the channel selector, hunting for the frequency the Russians were using. Kaufman found it. He said, "Got it, I think. One twenty-eight point nine."

Morgan set his selector, heard nothing at first. Then hard in his ear burst an unintelligible sentence with the characteristic fruity diphthongs of Russian. "I think that's it," he said.

He watched, and the satellite increased in size. "No rifle or any other weapon that I see," said Morgan. "But they *are* carrying a lot of extra oxygen bottles."

Kaufman grunted. McNary asked, "Can you tell if it's a collision course yet? I can't."

Morgan stared at the satellite through narrowed eyes, frowning in concentration. "I think not. I think it'll cross our bow twenty or thirty feet out; close but no collision."

McNary's breath sounded loud in the helmet. "Good. Then we've nothing but the men to worry about. I wonder how those boys pitch."

Another burst of Russian came over the radio, and with it Morgan felt himself slip into the relaxed state he knew so well. No longer was the anticipation rising. He was ready now in a state of calm, a deadly and efficient calm—ready for the test. This was how it always was with him when the time came, and the time was now.

Morgan watched as the other satellite approached. His feet were apart and his head turned sideways over his left shoulder. At a thousand yards, he heard a mutter in Russian and saw the man at the stern start moving rapidly toward the bow. His steps were long. Too long.

Morgan saw the gap appear between the man and the surface of the other ship, saw the legs kicking in a futile attempt to establish contact again. The radio was alive with quick, short sentences, and the two men turned and began to work their way swiftly toward the bit of human jetsam that floated near them.

"I'll be damned," said Kaufman. "They'll never make it."

Morgan had seen that this was true. The gap between floating man and ship widened faster than the gap between men and floating man diminished. Without conscious thought or plan, Morgan leaned forward and pulled the jack on the telephone line from McNary's helmet. He leaned back and did the same to Kaufman, straightened and removed his own. He threw a quick knot and gathered the line, forming a coil in his left hand and one in his right, and leaving a large loop floating near the ship in front of him. He stepped forward to clear Kaufman, and twisted his body far around to the right. There he waited, eyes fixed on the other satellite. He crouched slightly and began to lean forward, far forward. At the proper moment he snapped both his arms around to throw the line, the left hand throwing high, the right low. All his sailor's skill went into that heave. As the other satellite swept past, the line flew true to meet it. The floating man saw it coming and grabbed it and wrapped it around his hand and shouted into the radio. The call was not needed; the lower portion of the line struck one of the walking men. He turned and pulled the line into his arms and hauled it tight. The satellite was barely past when the bit of human jetsam was returning to its metallic haven. The two men became three again, and they turned to face the American satellite. As one man the three raised both arms and waved. Still without thinking, Morgan found himself raising an arm with Kaufman and McNary and waving back.

He dropped his arm and watched the satellite shrink in size. The calmness left him, replaced by a small spot of emptiness that grew inside him, and grew and swelled and threatened to engulf him.

Passage was ended, but the taste in his mouth was of ashes and not of glory.

His First Flight

LIAM O'FLAHERTY

"*When the bird descends with a great slant without beating its wings, the extremities of wings and tail bend upwards, and this movement is slow, for the bird is not only supported by the air beneath, but by the lateral air towards which the convex surface of the bent feathers spreads itself at equal angles*"—*from the notebooks of da Vinci. And this present story, it might be said, is how man's yearning to fly originated. He watched the birds in flight and set about imitating them—as we have seen.*

The young sea-gull was alone on his ledge. His two brothers and his sister had already flown away the day before. He had been afraid to fly with them. Somehow, when he had taken a little run forward to the brink of the ledge and attempted to flap his wings, he became afraid. The great expanse of sea stretched down beneath, and it was such a long way down—miles down. He felt certain that his wings would never support him, so he bent his head and ran away to the little hole under the ledge where he slept at night.

Even when each of his brothers and his little sister, whose wings were far shorter than his own, ran to the brink, flapped their wings, and flew away, he failed to muster up courage to take that plunge which appeared to him so desperate. His father and mother had come around calling to him shrilly, upbraiding him, threatening to let him starve on his ledge

249

LIAM O'FLAHERTY

unless he flew away. But for the life of him he could not
move.

That was twenty-four hours ago. Since then nobody had
come near him. The day before, all day long he had watched
his parents flying about with his brothers and sister, perfect-
ing them in the art of flight, teaching them how to skim the
waves and how to dive for fish. He had, in fact, seen his older
brother catch his first herring and devour it, standing on a
rock, while his parents circled around raising a proud cackle.
And all the morning the whole family had walked about on
the big plateau mid-way down the opposite cliff, taunting
him with his cowardice.

The sun was now ascending the sky, blazing warmly on
his ledge that faced the south. He felt the heat because he
had not eaten since the previous nightfall. Then he had
found a dried piece of mackerel's tail at the far end of his
ledge. Now there was not a single scrap of food left. He had
searched every inch, rooting among the rough, dirt-caked
straw nest where he and his brothers and sister had been
hatched. He even gnawed at the dried pieces of spotted
egg-shell. It was like eating part of himself.

He had then trotted back and forth from one end of the
ledge to the other, his grey body the colour of the cliff, his
long grey legs stepping daintily, trying to find some means of
reaching his parents without having to fly. But on each side
of him the ledge ended in a sheer fall of precipice, with the
sea beneath. And between him and his parents there was a
deep, wide chasm.

Surely he could reach them without flying, if he could only
move northwards along the cliff-face? But then, on what
could he walk? There was no ledge, and he was not a fly.
And above him he could see nothing. The precipice was
sheer, and the top of it was perhaps further away than the
sea beneath him.

250

He stepped slowly out to the brink of the ledge, and, standing on one leg with the other leg hidden under his wing, he closed one eye, then the other, and pretended he was falling asleep. Still they took no notice of him. He saw his brothers and his sister lying on the plateau dozing, with their heads sunk into their necks. His father was preening the feathers on his white back. Only his mother was looking at him.

She was standing on a little high hump on the plateau, her white breast thrust forward. Now and again she tore at a piece of fish that lay at her feet, and then scraped each side of her beak on the rock. The sight of the food maddened him. How he loved to tear food that way, scraping his beak now and again to whet it! He uttered a low cackle. His mother cackled too, and looked over at him.

"Ga, ga, ga," he cried, begging her to bring him over some food. "Gawl-ool-ah," she screamed back derisively. But he kept calling plaintively, and after a minute or so he uttered a joyful scream. His mother had picked up a piece of the fish and was flying across to him with it. He leaned out eagerly, tapping the rock with his feet, trying to get nearer to her as she flew across. But when she was just opposite to him, abreast of the ledge, she halted, her legs hanging limp, her wings motionless, the piece of fish in her beak almost within reach of his beak.

He waited a moment in surprise, wondering why she did not come nearer, and then, maddened by hunger, he dived at the fish. With a loud scream he fell outwards and downwards into space. His mother had swooped upwards. As he passed beneath her he heard the swish of her wings.

Then a monstrous terror seized him and his heart stood still. He could hear nothing. But it only lasted a moment. The next moment he felt his wings spread outwards. The wind rushed against his breast feathers, then under his stomach and against his wings. He could feel the tips of his wings cutting through the air. He was not falling headlong now. He was soaring gradually downwards and outwards. He was no longer afraid. He just felt a bit dizzy. Then he flapped his wings once and he soared upwards.

He uttered a joyous scream and flapped them again. He soared higher. He raised his breast and banked against the wind. "Ga, ga, ga. Ga, ga, ga. Gawl-ool-ah." His mother swooped past him, her wings making a loud noise. He answered her with another scream. Then his father flew over him screaming. Then he saw his two brothers and sister flying around him, curvetting and banking and soaring and diving.

Then he completely forgot that he had not always been able to fly, and commenced himself to dive and soar and curvet, shrieking shrilly.

He was near the sea now, flying straight over it, facing out over the ocean. He saw a vast green sea beneath him, with little ridges moving over it, and he turned his beak sideways and crowed amusedly. His parents and his brothers and sister had landed on this green floor in front of him. They were beckoning to him, calling shrilly. He dropped his legs to stand on the green sea. His legs sank into it. He screamed with fright and attempted to rise again, flapping his wings. But he was tired and weak with hunger and he could not rise, exhausted by the strange exercise. His feet sank into the green sea, and then his belly touched it and he sank no farther.

He was floating on it. And around him his family was screaming, praising him, and their beaks were offering him scraps of dog-fish.

He had made his first flight.